# Days Without Weather

—

Also by Cecil Brown

*The Life and Loves of Mr. Jiveass Nigger*

# Days Without Weather

# Weather

—

## CECIL

## BROWN

——

**Farrar Straus Giroux**
**New York**

The lines from Melvin B. Tolson's *Harlem Gallery*,
copyright © 1965 by
Twayne Publishers, Inc., are reprinted with the permission of
Twayne Publishers, a division of G. K. Hall & Company,
Boston, Massachusetts

The lines from "The River" are reprinted from
*The Complete Poems and Selected Letters and Prose of Hart Crane*,
edited by Brom Weber, copyright © 1933, 1966 by
Liverwright Publishing Corporation;
reprinted by permission of Liverwright Publishing Corporation

*Library of Congress Cataloging in Publication Data*
*Brown, Cecil. Days without weather.*
*I. Title.   PS3552.R6853D3   1983*
*813'.54   82-2392   AACR2*

*For my three sisters, Vivian, Brenda, and Elaine.*
*For Melissa—thank you for sticking it out.*
*And for Bea with love*

# Night: Sun
# Shiniest Day

———

*Why place an empty pail*
*before a well*
*of dry bones?*
*Why go to Nineveh to tell*
*the ailing that they ail?*

M. B. Tolson

# 1

I T was dark. The laughter and the dried smell of cigarette smoke and sound of jangled ice cubes and shuffling of feet and whispered undertones hit you as soon as you entered the room, which was now packed tight as one piece of flesh.

The Comedy City Improvisational Club—CCI—on Santa Monica Boulevard in Los Angeles didn't have a dressing room for its singers and comedians. You had to be content with a broom closet and a washbowl that would have been more at home in the Greyhound Bus Depot. For a mirror, there was a slab of cracked glass hanging precariously over the dirty washbowl.

Watching my face in the mirror, I lit another cigarette. Beyond the thin walls I could hear the spasmodic laughter, rising and falling, breaking like gushing waves on a jagged shore, and then the wheezy sound of an asthmatic seagull gliding lonely over the iron-gray seascape. And though this laughter contained much joy, when you heard it from a broom closet far away, you realized how awfully sad human laughter really is. Like the outlines of a picture on the wall, a stillness framed the loud chatter, and made me think of the word "humanity." Sometimes when I was listening to the laughter, and I couldn't see or hear the comedian, I would feel sorry for people. At least I would—and I could only speak for myself.

My name is Jonah, and I was twenty-two years old then, about six feet, a bit on the skinny side, though I really did have broad shoulders. Born and raised in Waycross, Georgia,

I went to a Southern college, graduated (finally), spent a summer doing street comedy at San Francisco State and Berkeley, was arrested (under a 1968 Free Speech Law), and then with my uncle's help beat it down here to L.A. That had been six months ago then. I had been doing stand-up since then. I did not like it, I preferred street comedy, but I didn't like that trip to jail, and for the first few weeks in that wicked city of Nineveh I did silent mime at the Los Angeles Museum right in front of the Balzac monument, amid the pigeon shit and peanut shells. But then I figured, "Let God's Will Be Done!" and started getting some jokes together. It wasn't what I wanted to do to wake people up, but I had to start somewhere.

From my broom closet, I listened to the audience howl like a wind. I SAW the faces, though I was not there. When the M.C., Dap Sugar, introduced Robbin—"A Young Comedian from New York Whom You've Seen on the *Tonight* Show— Ladies and Gentlemen Give a Warm Welcome to—" I saw exactly what she was wearing. After you'd done the same joke a million times, you began to see through walls.

Onstage, Robbin was taking the mike from its stand. Robbin was some sight. She had a face that put you in mind of the Skull and Cross you see on iodine bottles. She must've reached way down in the trash can to come up with that old raggedy gray pullover and those funky rags that use to be blue jeans about a million years ago. For hair she had this droopy brown moss that dripped down her skull like ham gravy. Her shape was on the thin side. In fact, it was a flagpole, but where she was suppose to have flags, she had these what looked like buttons beneath the tightly fitted sweater.

"Men say to me, why don't your tits stand up?" she said to the audience. "Now, isn't that a stupid, male-chauvinist, sexist thing to say, ladies? I tell them, IF YOU CAN GET YOUR

4 |

COCK TO STAND UP ALL THE TIME, I'll get my TITS TO STAND UP ALL THE TIME!!"

The house looked good. They stared at Robbin as if they were not sure if she was funny or not. Only the Omaha girls were into it. To tell you the truth, they were shrieking their corn-pone asses off.

Meanwhile, on stage, Robbin had gotten herself into a shouting match with a heckler. What happened was, she was telling this story about her sex life and left herself too open. A mistake comics frequently make.

"People've often wondered about my sex life," she said. " 'Robbin,' they say, 'who do you like making love with?' "

"With vibrators!"

A heckler had seen an open gap and, seizing the opportunity, had slipped in. A masculine voice, over in the dark corner of the room, the heckler was a guy with big biceps in a white T-shirt.

Robbin didn't miss a beat.

"Oh, you faggots, shut up!"

Like hurling a Frisbee over her shoulder, she sent the insult sailing over the heads to its destiny in the dark corner.

The two girls from Omaha shrieked with joy over this interchange.

"Dyke!" the heckler shot back.

"Faggots!"

Unfazed, the heckler went on: "You slit-slobbering muff-diver!"

"You cock-suckers keep quiet while I'm up here, okay?" Robbin fired back at them.

She barely got off stage with her composure. Dap Sugar quickly came to the stage and introduced Jack White to cool everybody out.

Jack White was wearing a green knit T-shirt and a pair of faded blue jeans. You would've never guessed his daddy was one of the board members of IBM. He started throwing his blond hair from his eyes. He was out for the All-American look. You could tell.

Hooking a thumb into the loophole of his jeans, Jack said, "Thank you, Dap, for that fine introduction—with introductions like that, you *need conclusions. . . .*"

The audience laughed and he went on: "I use to work back in Dallas with the juvenile delinquents. And I'd always run into these kids that'd robbed some old lady, or snatched some old lady's purse, or raped somebody, or held up a store. What amazed me was the reasons these kids gave for their crimes. Like there was this black kid. I'd say, 'Rufus, why did you rape that woman?' He'd say, *'Man, see, hit wuz lak uh dis! See man, I didn't uh rape 'er, I jest made 'er gib me some haid!'* "

The house snickered with him as he poked fun at the ignorance of the poor and black. Some people just laughed outright.

Only *white* comics like Jack White could get away with racial-dialect humor nowadays. If I made a joke like that, nobody'd laugh. They'd say I was bitter. If I used a swearword, they'd say I was imitating Billy Badman. Being a black comic was just a piece of hard luck.

I sat there feeling pretty depressed. Once I got on the stage, I kept telling myself, everything would be all right. Get it off my chest.

Jack White went off stage and Dap introduced Fatso Mitchell. "Ladies and gentlemen, welcome the comedy of Fatso Mitchell!"

Fatso came on and ribbed the audience with a mean stare —giving them time enough to take in his gargantuan vastness and to howl at his volume.

"I'm a goddamn shit-kicker and I just got kicked out of the KKK."

Then he took a beer out of a six-pack, bit the cap off with

his teeth, poured the beer into a glass, tilted it up to his mouth, gripping it between his teeth, threw his head back, and gulped down the contents.

Then: "Ladies and gentlemen, will you welcome the humor and comedy of the Love Songs of J. Alfred Prufrock!"

Master of High Camp Prufrock danced onstage.

"How many of you saw *Roots*, Part One?" he asked and didn't pause for their response. "Well, that damn movie almost ruined my life! I live, you know, in a white neighborhood and when *Roots* came out my neighbor wouldn't leave my blackass alone. They were pounding on my door in the middle of the night. *Aaaahhhhh! Let us in! We're sorry, we didn't mean to do it! Ahhh! Forgive us, forgive us. Please forgive us!* They were bringing me gifts, and every damn thing else. Finally, I just had to move, so I did . . . I moved to a whiter neighborhood . . . and then came *Roots*, Part Two! . . . And the shit started all over again. The phone would ring . . . I'd pick it up . . . Hello, Kunta Kinte speaking . . . It was them again! I said, 'Where is that goddamn Brady Bunch, when I need them! . . .' "

Pausing, he took a sip of the drink he was holding, and gave the audience time to laugh and applaud.

The audience laughed and clapped and smirked and simpered.

"But then I saw this movie called *The Great White Shark*. I said to myself, 'Now goddamnit, this is too much. As big as that ocean is out there, there's got to be a ghetto out there somewhere! Now where is *The Big Black Shark?*' "

I took a sip of my drink and absently watched Prufrock do his routine.

Sitting in that closet, I had my own special problem: my job required that I give them something unexpected, and each night I did not fail to do it. I had to surprise them, and in order to do that, I had to surprise myself. Otherwise, I'd've died of boredom. It was this seeking for the unexpected, the surprise, that made the job bearable. Yet I felt if I ever broke completely out of my routine, I would be a true artist, but I couldn't let go of my persona, my stage character. Don't ask me why, just accept the fact that I had not yet "found myself."

"Anyway, I've been up here long enough for my nigger friends to have stolen your cars," Prufrock said onstage. This was his closing joke. Now it was me! What's my routine?

Prufrock left the stage and Dap Sugar came on.

"We want to close our show tonight," he began, "with a new headliner . . . !" My heart sank and I nearly pissed on myself.

I started going over my routine in my head again for the umpteenth time. Except, believe it or not, suddenly my mind went blank. All of a sudden, just before I'm about to close the damn show, moments before my Big Moment, I couldn't remember anything of my routine. "Calm down," I thought, "calm down." I kept right on shaking like a madman.

Then Dap Sugar did this awful thing, something I'll never as long as I draw breath forgive him for. He gave me *a carnival show introduction* . . .

"Ladees 'n Gen'meeeeeens: De court JESTER un CAHmedy. GiVA BIIIEEEEGg round ah apPLAUS fer de MANNN who MADE DA WHALE lauFF. FUNNy MAN hisSELF. JONAH DrinkwahTUR!"

My first impulse was to run out of the club, run down the street, and run all the way back to the South. "De Mann who MADE DA WHALE LAUFF!"—I'd never heard anything like that!

What happened after this and how I got up on stage I cannot remember, but I was up there looking out. My prayer bones were knocking so loud they sounded like the dice in the hands of a Harlem crapshooter. I felt this tension in my breadbasket, and my mouth went dry as the dust in a tobacco field in July. The sea of laughing white faces. Yet I felt confident and exuberant. All my depression left me, my spirit soared high this time as it does each time I stand before an audience.

For a moment I experienced the sensation that I might not connect with the audience, but it was only for a moment. As soon as my feet touched the stage I started acting.

Let me back up forty-five feet and explain something. Like every comic in this business, I had a routine to fall back on in case of a pinch. But that night was one of those in which nothing came to me. When I stepped out on that stage my mind was blank as a sheet of typing paper, a *tabula rasa*. Baby, if you had asked me what my own *name* was, I probably would have said, "George Goebel." And meant it, too. That's how far into outer space my brain had drifted. Anyway, I had my routine divided into these three big categories that corresponded roughly—and I do mean roughly—into a beginning, middle, and end. The beginning I called "cold openings." In this part, if there's anything right on the audience's mind, I crack a joke about it right off. If there's been a recent scandal with some actor or some producer caught stealing the studio blind, or if a famous actor is getting a divorce or got raped and robbed, or a famous government agent turned out to be a Russian impersonator, or a black woman is killed in the ghetto because she didn't pay her light bill, I fire it out at the audience right away. I quip at anything that either shows the rich and famous enjoying more luck than they deserve or shows the poor suffering a stroke of misfortune more than they can bear.

The reason I do this is to find out what kind of audience is in the house. If my audience is white, I mock black people; if my audience is black, I'll use the same jokes but reverse them so I'm poking fun at whites. If the audience is mixed, I'll scoff at racists, hard hats, Ronald Reagan, and ignorant hillbillies. If my audience is white racists, I'll jeer at the hippies, the Black Panthers, Berkeley, California, liberals, Patty Hearst, *Ms.* magazine, and so forth on. A Southern,

Baptist democrat, I observe the same practice with religion and sex. If my audience is male, I scoff so much at women that people mistake me for a misogynist.

Now, after I've cased out the audience with my cold openings, I then go into the second part, "strutting my stuff." In this part, I develop the age-old premise that comics have been using since Aristophanes: people like to laugh at their neighbor (who lives in the adjoining towns or cities or countries). For example, I'll tell my audience I've been traveling, and while mocking the out-of-towners, I'll praise the citizens of the town I'm in. If I'm in San Diego, I'll make fun of people in L.A. If I'm performing in L.A., I'll say I just got back from San Diego and that all the people I met in San Diego were "assholes!" Everybody who lives in L.A. will laugh. In fact, I have a joke that goes like this: "What's an asshole?" "An asshole is anybody who lives in Los Angeles." When I tell this joke in a nightclub in San Francisco, do their jaws get wide and do their heels go into the air!

Then I do a number on farting. If the audience is into it by now I pull out my farting routine, which sounds like somebody reading Chapter 5 of Rabelais's *Gargantua*. Every comic can do farting jokes. Some are, naturally, better than others, but I find that most of the jokes come from setting up the situation where the farting takes place. I have a bit where I describe the preacher letting out a few SBD's (Silent But Deadly) while he's marrying a couple. After the farting routine, I do some Reagan jokes. I tell them Reagan is going back into the film business. I tell them that he is so old that the last birthday cake had so many candles on it, it looked like a brushfire. Next, I do a number called "Masturbation by the Numbers" in which I ask people how many of them masturbate. I play around with it for a bit. Next, I do a bit on TV commercials and Folger's coffee.

By now I'm in the third part of my routine: "the closings." In my closings I have several choices, "Stories from My

Southern Childhood" or "Animals Making Love." In "Stories" I do black Southern folklore jokes like about the White man, the Jew, and the Black man. In "Animals" I mime all the various animals making out; I do their facial expressions and I even imitate the sounds of grunting chairs and sticks and stones make. (Master of prosopopoeia here!)

Going to the mike, I decided to do the scene of the Pimp Getting into His Cadillac parked on the corner. I began to imitate the Cadillac sitting on the curb. Then I did him getting inside. They had the image of the Cadillac so perfectly clear in mind that they laughed at their own recognition.

I realized that I was halfway into my routine and hadn't done any of my standard material. I felt I was losing my liberals, my homosexuals, and my show-biz producer. Sure, I could make the brothers and sisters laugh all night, but they weren't the ones who were going to hire me for a television series. I had to get those show-biz guys and their dates laughing.

I paused for the laughter, which was considerable. I felt high then. "Nothing can stop me," I thought. Just have to wait for the spur of the moment, the unexpected surprise. *Go back to the Folger's coffee commercial,* I'm telling myself. *What about TV . . ."*

"What about TV . . . Isn't TV the absolute pits these days?"

Good response to that one. Great applause from the liberals. *Now move on to the next one. Carol Lawrence and the Hills Bros coffee commercial.*

"But my favorite coffee commercial is Carol Lawrence and the Hills Bros coffee commercial. Now the key to this little gem is that Carol Lawrence is really a hooker . . ."

"Hahahahaha!" A woman laughed.

". . . That's *right!*"

". . . Funny!" Somebody else clapped.

". . . Why else does she always have a man in her house

late at night? Why else does she always have on a night-
gown? And have you noticed, all of these men are 'just an old
friend'? That bitch is sellin' something . . . and it *ain't coffee!*"
I paused for the laugh.

"Hohoaha!"

Timing is a comic's greatest asset.

I saw the girl with the Omaha hairdo laugh and nudge the
other one, the fatter one.

"I don't think he's that funny." She laughed.

I saw the liberal in the neat, expensive suit smile faintly.
The beautiful young girl sitting beside him squeezed his
hand under the table. And as if this was not enough, they
looked at each other and smiled. What a smile, too! What a
success he was! What a wonderful man for her to marry!
Such a lovely couple.

"Hahaha!" I saw the sister with a head full of cornrows
and a shiny gold-tooth laugh.

"Hehehehe!" I heard one of the Santa Monica faggots grin.
*Do "Animals Making Love" now. And then the "Stories
from My Southern Childhood."*

"Now I'd like to do my impression of various animals making love," I started . . . "Here's how rabbits make love," I said.
I sprinted across the stage and humped the air quickly as I
ran. Humping the air, I watched their laughing faces. So
innocent. Childish. Stupid. Gross. Human. Just people.

"Hoho," I heard the sister with the cornrows again. I could
see the liberals smiling and the Omaha girls.

"Snakes don't have sex organs," I said, "but they screw
just the same. Do you know how they do it? Well, the female
snake just open her mouth . . ." I opened my mouth and
rolled my eyes.

". . . and the dude snake just crawls right into it and do his
thing and comes on out again . . ."

Nothing came. I went on, hoping for something morally
edifying.

12 |

"But the two animals that I get a kick out of when they screw is the ant and the elephant. Have anybody ever had the privilege of seeing an elephant and an ant fucking . . . ?" I paused and then I went into my impression of an ant humping an elephant. "See, this ant had been in hibernation all winter . . ." I mimicked an ant coming out of a hole. I wiped my eyes like I've just gotten up out of bed. I stretched and yawned.

"Uh-uh-uh!" I gave the ant a human grunt, and to the side of the stage, I gave him a human voice. "What does the ant see?" I looked blankly at the audience and announced: "He sees Miss Elephant grazing grass. Goddamn, I want me some of *that!*"

"Hahahaha!" I heard somebody in the back laugh.

"So he runs over and starts humping the elephant like this!" I said, humping the air. I'm a comic named Jonah, who believes he's an ant fucking an elephant. "That's how ants fuck elephants!" Anybody silly enough to do this will get a laugh.

Then I do the elephant as she is about to have an orgasm. "This is the elephant!"

I buck my eyes and stretch my lips as wide as I can get them. I thought to myself, Stepin Fetchit, eat your heart out.

"OOOOHHHHH! *Oh, shit! I'm commin.'* " I imitated the elephant having an orgasm. I heard them laugh and that gave me the cue to finish the bit.

Then I finished the bit with a topper. I explained to them: "Well, one time the ant was screwing the elephant and a coconut fell out of a tree and knocked the elephant unconscious. The ant jumped off the pussy and started swaggering like a real macho. He looks down at the moaning elephant and says, 'Suffer, bitch, suffer!' "

As I imitated the ant I heard the house go wild; I grabbed my nuts and adjusted them, then jacked my pants up, hunched my shoulder, and said, "Yeah, bitch, suffer!" and that got my biggest laugh.

Everything was going fine. I was regaining my confidence. I knew that I could get the laughs I wanted, but something was missing. What was it?

Suddenly it came to me I had to do something surprising. Something that even the other comics didn't expect, something that would embarrass everybody. I kept looking for that moment . . . Meanwhile, I told them about my past under the guise of a title called "Southern Stories."

I was born in the South of sharecroppers. Thalia, the owner of the club, was standing at the back of the room laughing. She was laughing louder than anybody else. I thought to myself, *Now's the time to thank her for what she did for you.* On the spur of the moment, I decided to ask her to stand up and then I'd say, "Ladies and Gents, my Jewish Mother." But as the laughter subsided, Thalia's laughter was distinctively obvious.

"LADIES AND GENTLEMEN, I WOULD LIKE YOU TO MEET HER —MY MOTHER! . . ."

I made a slip and forgot to say *"Jewish* mother." I could tell that the audience would laugh at that.

"MY MOTHER JUST CAME ALL THE WAY OUT FROM GEORGIA TO SEE ME . . ."

". . . MOTHER, WOULD YOU PLEASE STAND UP . . ."

Joe was flashing the spotlight all over the place. He was a comic himself, and as soon as he sniffed humor he started panning the room with the spotlight until it fell on the proprietor of the club. "THERE SHE IS! MOTHER!" I gasped. Beneath the spotlight, Thalia looked like a Jewish refugee. They expected a black lady, one of those Sister Sadies. But there, standing under the glaring spotlight was a pale Jew.

". . . MOMS . . . WOULD YOU TAKE A BOW . . ."

Going along with the joke, Thalia stood up. Wow! Did they

laugh then. Joe put the spotlight on her and she actually stood up.

ZAP!—*Right in the kisser!* The audience saw the joke coming, but it was too late! I had them. Oh, did their eyes bulge! Did their mouths gape wide open! Did they chortle! *My Mother!* This white lady! You could just see them looking at me, thinking, *This shameless motherfreyer, no class, this guy! He'll do anything for a laugh.*

The whole house broke up. I saw Robbin laughing, and even Old Prufrock was grinning.

That's it, I thought, I'd make it. Just in time, too. I came off the stage and Thalia gave me a kiss.

"You were great," she said. I don't know if it was because she didn't understand what had happened or she just wanted to help me end my act, but she didn't seem to mind that I'd gotten a big joke off of her. Already I dreamed of laughing with the comics at Ben Franks. I said "Thanks." I headed for my car. I had to see my friend Buddy. We had been talking about developing an act, and tonight we were going to get together and discuss it again.

When I came outside I felt like a prisoner who'd been given a reprieve. Before I went on the stage, I felt frustrated and used. Now I was feeling new and light. I felt good. I really did.

As I was pulling my car out of the parking lot, Prufrock pulled up beside me in his white Jaguar.

"Brother," he said, with the window rolled down, "you pissed tonight! Yeah, you broke Thalia's face! And you got on everybody's case."

I was grinning so hard that I couldn't keep my mouth closed if my life depended on it. Then Prufrock said, "Meet-'cha at Ben Franks!" and pulled off.

# 2

I pulled into the Ben Franks parking lot, sweethearted my raggedyass Fiat right between these gaudy fish-tailed Cadillacs, and went inside.

Ben Franks is this hangout for L.A. comics, mainly for broke comics, and since black comics were the broke comics, mainly black comics went there. They'd come from clubs right down the street like the L.A. Connection on Hollywood Boulevard and the Off the Wall on Fairfax and the Comedy Café on La Cienega and as far away as the New Ice House way out Mentor Avenue in Pasadena.

As you entered the joint, there was a string of vendor machines replenished with the copious pornographic rag-sheets for jacking off in the bathrooms, at least that's what the bathroom smelled like. The ratty, well-worn welcome mat at the entrance was hardly ever taken notice of by the thousands of diverse people that trod over it. Nevertheless, it should've been replaced by the sign which Gargantua put over the door of his Theleme: DO WHAT YOU WILL. For the comics who went there acted as if they were the original Thelemites. We could do or say whatever we liked, for we were the comics: and we got away with it, too. This comic license drew other "crazies" to our hangout, so that it wasn't long before "straight" people started coming to the place to gawk at us.

The place was swarming with bleary-eyed punk rockers and hookers from the Strip and cops on a break and grifty pickpockets looking for marks and comics and the varicose-legged waitresses, grandmothers in white aprons. There was a table full of straight-looking society people looking me dead in the eye. Every night here was the same. Some hooker would always cuss out one of the waitresses, who, too stupid or tired to argue, would bring in the manager. The manager, having done this for the scumpteenth time, would schlepp out and give this unconvincing performance of pretending that the hooker had offended the policy of the place ("What policy?") and would ask the hooker to leave. The hooker would summarily cuss out the manager, at which point the comics would take an active role in defending the hooker against the callous insensitivity of the management. (It's hard, I know, to imagine a comic defending anybody . . .) The hooker would also cuss out the policeman called to throw her out. The policeman would rarely throw her out, though. After she cussed him out, the hooker would leave and the policeman would go back to his coffee and his conversation with his partner.

While all this would be going on, the comics would be collecting material, scrutinizing the incident for any absurdities that might make a repressed audience laugh. "Looking for stuff," we would say. We would laugh at the hookers and the waitresses and the cops and not infrequently a funny line would end up in somebody's act on stage. "I found some new stuff that worked," you'd hear some comic say.

With its orange vinyl seats and plastic tables, Ben Franks was a way station, a club, and a school. A large corner table was reserved for us. There was a smaller table next to it which the white comics sat at. Even the Chinese comedian Gilbert Wong and the Indian comedian Charlie Horse shied away from our table. The white comics, "Society Boys," we called them, were the very spirit of conservatism. Whooping and yelling, we black comics would be woodshedding verbal

voodoo and exercising our self-hating, mordant wit by playing the "dozens," "cutting," "reading," and "ranking" each
other with so much jive the white comics always turned red
trying to figure out when we were being serious and when we
were only kidding. When we got to cussing each other out,
the white squares would expect to see razors come out. Slice
City. Then we would start laughing. They couldn't figure it
out, and so they kept their distance.

I sweethearted a chair at the table with Winfield, Fullhouse, Buddy, Prufrock. Only one other person was missing
for our game to begin: Mr. John Stubbs, and nothing really
got started until he arrived.

"You anywhere, Fishman?" Winfield asked me as I slid in
beside them. Winfield was a handsome yellow black man
with light green eyes in his forties. Dressed in an expensive
purple silk shirt, his eyes at half-mast either from no sleep
or drugs (no doubt both), he sketched a drawing of Prufrock
on his pad which he carried with him everywhere. (Other
drawings of the Hollywood Wits Club members were on the
wall behind us.) A pickpocket, Winfield usually amazed us
with hard-luck stories told in the exciting argot of the under-
world, but when he came to perform on the stage, they would
all dissolve. Now he never went on the stage any more. His
main act was "life" in big capitalized letters. His sad stories
were funny but he wasn't.

"Winfield," Prufrock said to him, glancing down at the
drawing, which began to take on the likeness of the elegant,
sweet-smelling master of the razor wit, who could cut so fast
that his victim would still be laughing, the lips still turned
up in a smile, when his head fell off. Disdaining the word
"comic," Prufrock saw himself as a great actor. Like a shark,
he swam deep into the sea world of the movie stars and knew
their sex lives so intimately that his cutting humor had as
many levels as Dante's *Divine Comedy*. Living off the lady
lovers of his comedy, he measured their appreciation of his

"genius" by the amount of money he found in their purse when he departed with it.

"Winfield," he said, "you have a great gift for comedy, but you must give up your old habits."

Prufrock uncorked a genie with those words. Fullhouse and Buddy began to laugh, sensing a put-down.

"What habits?" Fullhouse asked, turning to Prufrock. Fullhouse was a hundred-percent Negro with a tree trunk for a body and a head as empty as a house after the furniture has been repossessed by the finance man. A dullard, his main job was as an "instructor" at the Jack La Lanne spa, where he was known as the "comic" among the weight lifters. (Among us comics he was known as a "weight lifter.") His sense of humor suffered from arrested development and remained on the same level as *Hustler* magazine, which, of course, he thought was as subtle in its humor as *The New Yorker*. I remembered one of his jokes about some little kids eating shit that was frozen into the form of a popsicle. Fullhouse would stand on stage and roll his eyes with innocent relish just like a little kid. Embarrassing but not embarrassed himself, he got great laughs off that bit, which he later told me was "inspired" by his reading of *Hustler* magazine. He added that he had been "called to perform," just as a preacher is "called to preach."

"Oh, he knows what they are," Prufrock teased, "white women and drugs."

"You gonna let Prufrock talk about you like that," Buddy signified. A medium-complexioned black man in his early thirties, a doctor's son, Buddy always liked to think of himself as being one of the blacks who came up the hard way. An existential black humorist, he felt every one of his jokes had to carry a "revolutionary message" like a cyanide-coated bullet. People who didn't take the time to understand him thought he was out to kill people with his humor, but his jokes were really about stealing. A black

Robin Hood of the ghetto was his image of himself. He sat there dressed in a blue Chairman Mao cap, a plaid shirt and worn denims.

"Winfield," Prufrock went on with his verbal torture, while we beat the table and slapped our knees, "haven't I seen you so fucked up that you were down on your knees sniffing up this white woman's dress? Now tell the truth, nigger. We're all friends here."

"Yeah, I was lookin' under a woman's dress," Winfield said, handing Prufrock the drawing he did of him. "But it was yo' mamma's!"

"Ho, ho, ho!" Buddy chortled. "Nigger's playing the dozens again!"

"Don't play the dozens, man. Y'all might hurt Prufrock's delicate feelings." Fullhouse laughed. "He's gay, you know."

"Oh, I am? Am I?" Prufrock miffed, looking at Winfield's image of him. "I guess this looks like me."

"Yeah, a black Oscar Wilde," I said, fueling Fullhouse's joke. "If you ain't gay, you're standing in the Soon-to-Be-Gay line. When the next gay dies, you'll be next."

"That's great, Fishman," Buddy said, rewarding me with a slap on the back and a laugh.

Just as Lois, the black waitress, set down a batch of pancakes for the Hollywood Wits and Chinese tea for Prufrock, we noticed some strange goings-on at the dining counter. A sex-change case, a six-footer dressed in a long black wig, a brown skirt with a slit up one side, and fishnet stockings, was having an argument with a drunk. I felt sorry for her. Prufrock turned his nose up at it. Buddy lamented it. Winfield didn't laugh, either, but Fullhouse thought it was very funny, especially when the drunk started asking the sex change for a date.

"That's a great scene," Fullhouse laughed. "I'm getting some great stuff."

"Well, if I can't have a date," the drunk blurped, "how about a kiss! All you hookers are alike."

"I'm not a hooker," the sex change said.

"You ain't no hooker"—the drunk hiccuped—"because you ain't no woman. You're a man! Heh! heh! heh!"

"Kiss my pussy, you insensitive person!" she shrieked.

"You ain't gotta pussy! Drag queens don't have pussy unless the doctors tuck some flesh and fold it."

"How disgusting you men are. How disgusting! I've never heard anything as disgusting," she went on like some dicty broad.

"Where is your pussy then?"

"You want to see my pussy? You want to see my pussy?" When she reached down to pull up her skirt I looked away, and I saw Mr. Stubbs stroll in. Immaculately togged in a tailored double-breasted pin-stripe and a polka-dot bowtie and his head as clean-shaven as a garlic bud, he saw the woman with her skirt over her head and gasped.

"Jesus Christ! What's going on? What is this joint coming to?" he lamented. "I use to sit here with Lenny Bruce, but now look at the kind of things that takes place here; Lenny would be so disappointed."

Mr. Stubbs hobbled over to the table starting ranking us right away. "Hey, Fuckface!" he started off. A well-known television comedian whose career began with smutty records before he was discovered by the mass media, Mr. Stubbs was the comedian emeritus. Because he was always full of comical insults, we never felt brought down in his company. It was very hip, in fact, to match wits with him. That's how most of us stayed sharp. Rabelais reincarnated, he was past master of cataloging obscenities.

When he talked about farts, shitting, snot races, and wiping his ass our stomachs trembled and shook and begged for mercy. Just by the tone of his voice, his nasty tone of voice,

| 21

his benign facial expressions, his unconsciousness—he made us laugh.

Like Santa Claus distributing small gifts to little children, Mr. Stubbs handed each of us his daily insult. Reading left to right, he started with Winfield; nodding at him, he said epigrammatically: "See what happens when the embryo gets too much oxygen!"

We laughed as one. Next, it was Fullhouse's turn.

"Fullhouse," he said, "you're so ugly, nigger! Every time I look at you I think of your great-great-great-great-grand *pappa*, that Watusi Warrior, and then I think of your great-great-great-grand*mamma*, a big black *buffalo!* You're proof that the Africans did *fuck* the buffalo!"

Fullhouse, like Winfield before him, tried to come back. "Don't come round here with that antique jive!" he countered ineffectually.

Then he turned to read Prufrock. "Prufrock," he said, "they tell me you have a fast-paced delivery—for sucking cocks!"

Prufrock laughed it off.

Then he turned to me. "Jonah, you little corn-fed, country nigger, how did the white man let you get outa Mississippi!"

I felt my face crack with laughter, and I howled.

". . . Nigger, when Colonel Tom was jamming yo' great-grandmama behind the barn . . ."

". . . *Yo' hankerchief-headed, shuffling Uncle Tom,*" I joked back but Stubbs went on to Buddy.

"Buddy, you're the only comic in America who can say 'I just fucked a white woman' and make Ronald Reagan laugh," he jabbed at Buddy. "But what happened to you? You look like you didn't take your dosage of Thorazine today."

After that congenial introduction, Stubbs moved on to another one of our verbal games of wit-matching:

"White Comedy is an old sixty-five-year-old white woman that lost her virginity to a vibrator in the luggage compartment of an Amtrak train headed for Bitchville, Alabama! Black comedy is a turd in the constipated bowels of the Great White World!" he blabbed, baiting the other comics. "Can any of you Hollywood nitwits top that?"

"Lemme throw my pennies in with your dollars, boy," Winfield said, as he began to sketch Mr. Stubbs on the pad. "I don't know about white comedy, but black comedy is a black sonabitch born in an alley to a whore and a pimp!"

A geyser of laughter erupted and spilled over the table.

"That's funny, Winfield"—Buddy horselaughed—"but I'd say black comedy is the religion of laughing philosophers."

"Banzai!" cheered Prufrock. "It's the manna of the Negro in the Great White World!"

"It's dreaming with your eyes open," I metaphorized.

"Black comedy is a consumption that eats up white existence!" Fullhouse spat out.

"Black comedy is a living contradiction," Buddy observed, "because the life of a black comic ain't funny!"

"That he isn't funny—but very serious—is *very* funny!" Prufrock interposed smoothly, raising the curtains on the stage of a hard-to-catch insight. Applauding the curtain raiser with a smile, Buddy said, "White comedy is no match for black comedy. White comedy denies herself any fun, won't date anybody but Prince Charming. But black comedy is hot to trot! Before you can say Jack Rabbit, she's consumed herself with fun and has kicked out two or three little bastards of unknown paternity to prove it!"

We stomped our feet, slapped each other's back, and beat the table.

"We have a cause to give ourselves to," Buddy said solemnly and slammed his fist on the table. "But these white comics don't make any demands, make no promises, but raise every expectation, like a man in drag. But black comedy is a marriage between beautiful illusion and grim reality."

"Gents, the theme for tonight's discussion is: What should we, the Hollywood Wits, make fun of?" Winfield said. "This is a serious question. Pope John got shot! The President Reagan just got shot! All within a few weeks. Would it be in bad taste to make jokes about them? Yet if we don't, are we overlooking some very good material by observing these inhibiting niceties?"

"My feeling is that it would be inappropriate to refer to the President," Mr. Stubbs said.

"Stubbs, you must be crazy to give advice like that," Buddy said. "As much money as you've made telling dirty jokes, are you a Republican or something weird?"

"No, he's rich," Prufrock laughed. "When you got his kind of money, you're happy, and when you're happy, you got no problems, and when you got no problems, you ain't nigger any more. You're white! Ha, hahahahaha!" Winfield laughed.

"Let the audience decide what's funny," Buddy said. "People feel different about Reagan in different parts of the country. In Berkeley, you get on the stage and say, 'Reagan got shot,' they yell back, 'I hope he dies and goes to hell!' "

"Yeah, but people in Berkeley live in a marijuana coma," Stubbs said. "What do they know!"

"If Reagan went to hell they'd be a lot of niggers that he starved to death waiting in line to kick his ass!" Fullhouse laughed. "Imagine the look on Reagan's face when he met those twenty-three blacks that they killed down in Georgia."

"Each of us must find his own individual way of contributing to the whole of black comedy," Mr. Stubbs said. "It's like the colors in the rainbow. Each of us finds his own color in the rainbow of art. Find your own style and stop stealing the other man's jokes. Let that be each of our ambitions."

"My advice is to be humble," Buddy said. "The mystery of God is in the soul of the humble man. Duke Ellington said that, I believe it."

"What difference does any of this make?" Prufrock said. "The world is fallin' apart anyway."

"The most important thing is telling jokes that people want to buy," Stubbs said.

"No, it isn't," Buddy said. "The black bourgeoisie and the Great White World have forced the Negro comedian into a dichotomy. To be or not to be a Negro. That's the question."

"If you can't make any money, what difference does it make if you study your navel or not? What difference does it make if your navel is Negro or not?" Fullhouse asked.

"Anyway, I'm leaving," Buddy announced. "I can't live in a town that's dedicated to making people rich just because they're whites. Blacks are natural artists because we are not repressed with guilt like whites. Though naturally funny and talented, we can't make a living at it in this town. When we do, it's because *whites* think we are funny. We become whitenized. I refused to whitenize my art."

"Where are you going then?" I was surprised he was leaving. "What about our comedy team?"

"I received a letter from the dean of a small college in Santa Cruz not far from the sea," he said, smiling and stroking his moustache. "I'm going to take a position in the English department."

What a sad dude I must've looked like then! I depended on Buddy's friendship for encouragement. Now what he was telling us was he was going over the wall. It was tantamount to betrayal, or even treason.

"I decided that it was time for me to leave the city before my hair turns gray," he said sadly.

Prufrock took a sip of his tea.

"But why?" he asked.

"This city is no place for a decent man to live," Buddy said.

"Who except the rich can afford a decent place to live here? If you're corrupted enough, you can become rich. But how am I going to become rich? I'm not a sell-out to my race. I can't stand up on the *Tonight* show and whitenize my culture."

"Well, I'm rich, goddamn it, and I think that's the solution to the black man's problem," Mr. Stubbs came back. "Get the money and tell 'em to fuck themselves."

"That's a sorry solution," Buddy said.

"And what you want to do? Tear the system down?" Mr. Stubbs scowled. "But what about him?" he pointed to me. "You tear the system down and what happens to his hopes? He got a sister and mother and father back in Georgia that wants him to make it. You gonna deny him that opportunity to be somebody?"

"Everybody has a beef," Prufrock said, turning to me, too. "What's yours, Fishman?"

"I don't know who I am," I said. "I mean, what kind of comedian am I? I haven't 'found myself.' "

Mr. Stubbs rubbed his bald head and looked at one of the huge diamonds on his finger, addressed me. "You'll find yourself one day, Jonah," he said, "and when you do, nobody'll have to tell you that you have. You'll feel it in your bones. Just keep at it." And then he looked around. "Now let's get the hell outa here before the vice squad arrives."

The manager was trying to get the sex change out the door and the drunk, who, as it turned out, was a comedian, was trying to defend her "honor."

As we got up from the table, Winfield gave everybody his wallet back. He was a very good pickpocket, that guy.

A few minutes later Buddy and I walked out to the parking lot to his Peugeot.

"Goodbye, Jonah," he said. "I guess you'll have to get you another partner."

26 |

"I guess so," I said, "But I'll be okay, my uncle's getting me this job in one of his films."

But he wasn't really listening to me. He was already in Santa Cruz. "You take care, dude," he said. "Just keep laughing and you'll find yourself sooner than you think."

"Goodbye," I said, and I drove sadly back to Brentwood.

# 3

I parked the car in front of Uncle Gadge's house and went inside. The house was quiet and dark. I made it to my room and flicked on the light. Considering what a slob I am, my room is fairly neat. I had a poster of Bert Williams and one of Uncle Gadge's play *Black Christ* on the wall. I had a pretty good collection of comedy records, too. There was the Leonardo picture, "The Madonna and Saint Anne," over my bed.

I was more disturbed by admitting that I didn't know who I was professionally than by the actual situation. I suffered self-doubt very badly. Mr. Stubbs had encouraged me, I kept reminding myself. I had actually said it, but they didn't know just how true it was. "You cannot be famous until you've 'found yourself,' " my uncle once told me. One thing I knew, was that I was not just a black man. I wasn't just those things they said a black man was. I was more than that. I knew I was "man," but I didn't know what kind of man, to say nothing about what kind of comic I was.

So who was I?

I had a full-length mirror on the wall opposite the door so that I could practice my routines. I stood looking at myself in the mirror. What a different person I had become. I remembered waiting at the Los Angeles airport for my uncle to pick me up. I was coming off a flight from San Francisco, where I had been for the last three summer months. I had just gotten out of jail. I was broke but not discouraged. I was just amazed and shocked! Judging from the good looks of the people around me, I was in a movie. When I stepped on the sidewalk with my clothes in a Safeway shopping bag (I had already pawned the dark-brown Gucci, a graduation present from Uncle Gadge and Aunt Lottie), I discovered that the impression of the clean sidewalks and flower-filled street dividers played delightfully on my senses in a way I had never experienced in the East or South. Although I had just been living in San Francisco for three months, I wasn't prepared for the physical beauty of Southern California.

When I arrived in Los Angeles I must've looked like some square just out of college, but after running into such bad luck, I had to sell a few items—like my one really good jacket, the one piece of clothing I would put on when I wanted to look like a black boy who'd gone to college. Soon, I had replaced my rimless glasses with a pair of hip red ones. My uncle didn't recognize me.

When I passed a telephone booth, the girl who emerged from it was more attractive than any girl I'd seen in my whole life—or so it seemed at that moment. When I backed up, she smiled and I was certain that I'd seen her in a movie once.

"Jonah!" When I saw my uncle, I realized how much time had changed him. This happened six months ago—I was twenty-two, just out of college, and under those circumstances time seemed to work only on other people—especially uncles—and never me. Now, of course, I do not suffer that illusion. At my graduation, then a year ago, Uncle Gadge had surprised me when he showed up with other members of my family, and even then I was surprised at his relatively diminutive stature and the corporality of his being. He's my father's brother, but my father is thin and six feet. They both had those dark skins, with aquiline features, nappy hair, broad shoulders, thin behinds, and broad, flat feet—except my father is thin and tall and Uncle Gadge fat and round. My father is a farmer and my uncle is a TV and movie screenwriter.

Uncle Gadge put my luggage—such as it was—in the trunk of a dark-blue 450SL Mercedes-Benz and when I got in I thought of my father's shabby Chevrolet. You would be hard put to find two people as different as my father and my uncle. This difference has always been explained by my family as being due to the fact that my uncle went to college and my father stayed on the farm. My grandfather had a great deal of land and when he died my father stayed on to keep it up, but my uncle went North to school. My mother always told us that my uncle's people tricked my father out of his monetary inheritance. My uncle got more than his share of the money bequeathed the children, and it was on this money he went to college, and my father, the nicer of the two, not being a greedy person, was content to stay on the land. Odessa, my father's favorite sister, who possessed an unusual tenacity for clinging to the truth, went even further. She claimed that, egged on by the cloak-and-dagger ambition of the other side of his family, my uncle stole the ten thousand dollars due my father. My father claims that he bought his share of his brother's land as a way of explaining Uncle Gadge's educational advantage. At my graduation celebration, my father was on very good terms with Uncle Gadge and encouraged me to go to California to start my new life with him. In addition to his education, Uncle Gadge had won a reputation for a play presented in Greenwich Village during the late sixties. The play, which was based on the death of his younger brother Lindsey, had been a great critical success, coming as it did right on the crest of the black power movement. My uncle may not have talent but he sure has timing. First, he won an Obie award and was able to use it as a way of persuading a Hollywood studio to hire him as a screenwriter; one finally did and for the next few years we didn't hear from him although we did read about him in magazines like *Ebony.*

Lindsey's murder sent my father into the civil rights movement and my uncle, his brother, into the theater, and it marked the end of my boyhood days of innocence and the beginning of my youth.

Lindsey had been killed by a young white boy, a Martin, whom we had known all our lives.

I turned from the mirror and walked over to my bed. Perhaps, I thought, what Mr. Stubbs was hinting at was not what I was about at all. Perhaps what he was hinting at was something else. "You'll know when you've found yourself." Maybe he meant I had to develop another kind of comic hero.

Maybe there is something about this in my Bert Williams quote, I thought and went over to the window where my desk was. Over my desk I had scotch-taped a quote from the only essay Bert Williams ever wrote on comedy, entitled "The Comic Side of Trouble," published in *The American Magazine* (1917).

> If you observe your own conduct whenever you see a friend falling down on the street, you will find that nine times out of ten your first impulse is to laugh and your second is to run and help him up. To be polite you will dust off his clothes and ask him if he has hurt himself. But when it is over, all over, you can't resist telling him how funny he looked when he was falling. *The man with the real sense of humor is the man who can put himself in the spectator's place and laugh at his own misfortunes.*

I had it just above my desk, and every night when I went to bed and every morning when I got up, I looked at it. I tried to remember it when I would go on stage. I tried to tell all my stories as if they were the most horrible things that've ever happened to a man, and I told them as if I was about the most unlucky fellow in the world, and it didn't matter what I told, as long as I put on a poker face, and told it as if my own unhappiness was so absolute that I was indifferent to my own suffering. I had this one story I told, which actually happened to me, about when I was a little boy in the first grade and I asked Ruth Smith for some pussy. I didn't know what pussy was, I'd only heard my Uncle Lindsey talking about it. I thought it was something like an apple, and Ruth told the teacher and the teacher, Miss Williams, with whom I was naturally in love, took me into the closet to whip me with the switches I'd gotten her to whip the other first-graders. Well, the story is nothing; the comedy consists of *how* I told it. I made my situation so pitiful that I'm actually being shot by a firing squad. I would go into the drum roll like they do when they're about to shoot you down for treason. You see the blindfold as they put it on my eyes, you hear my trembling heart, the petrification of fear as it forces me to inadvertently piss on myself (. . . you see the piss pouring over my feet), you see the rifles go up (the switches raised), you see the soldiers take aim.

Take Aim!

Fire!

The pussy rebellion has been squashed! Order has been restored! Down with the pussy-askers! Down with SIX-YEAR-OLD PUSSY HOUNDS! I AM DEAD AND FOR WHAT? For asking for IT. Then I would do the teacher's "TRIUMPHANT SMILE."

But this is not what Mr. Stubbs meant, I thought. And besides, this comic hero was just another side of my multifaceted personality. Who was I? Well, I was everybody. I was whatever somebody else thought I was. I remembered one day when I went to Venice Beach with the fellows. Me and Prufrock, Fullhouse and Buddy piled into Buddy's beat-up Chevy and made it to the beach. It was hot and crowded. Buddy spent all of the time sitting at a café talking to this babe that ran the Venice Art Gallery. Fullhouse went straight over to where the weight lifters flex their muscles for the female spectators and after me and Prufrock went to get hot dogs, on our way back, we saw him lifting about a million pounds onto his mountainous black shoulders and his little bird-like head turning mechanically, looking into women's faces to see who was looking, smiling just like comics do on stage.

Prufrock and I sat on the sandy, bikini-clad beach listening to his tape recorder. The dude had taped the music from the movie *Jaws* and was playing it full volume. Suddenly white people started jumping out of the water when they heard that music. The music went, "DA—DUM! DA—DUM! DA—DUM!" We would walk up and down the beach and people would laugh and we had a great time with that joke. This one girl in this string bikini came up to me: "Are you a Leo?" I said, "Uh-huh!" With the way she was smiling at me and the sight of her big breasts peeping out of that bikini at me, what was I suppose to say? Back in Hollywood I went over to her place to see her. She was togged in white short-shorts and high-heeled slut shoes. We talked about Dante, went to a film, made love in every possible position. Every time I did something she really liked or really didn't like, she'd say: "Typical Leo!" Or: "Typical fucking Leo!" The next morning she said, "Leos have a great sex drive! You're such a Leo, I can't believe it." When I was leaving her apartment, the sun was falling very nicely in the doorway. She said: "When I saw you with that *Jaws* music, I said: 'Typical Leo!' "

I just sat on the bed thinking about her. I had never seen her again. How could I ever tell her that I wasn't a Leo at all. That was the big joke. I'm a Cancer. Ho-ho-ho! No doubt about it, if I told her that I'd lied to her about being a Leo she'd probably say: "Typical fucking Leo!"

So was that the real me who was saying I was a Leo when

I knew I was a Cancer? What does it mean to "find yourself?"

Perhaps there was something in my past that would help me "find myself." Some horrible deed. Something that, once remembered, would release me and I'd "know myself."

I tried to think of what this "something" was. Lindsey's death. I began to think about the Martin family.

The Martin family had once been an example of Southern Nobility and had owned a plantation on the Cape Fear River. In the early part of the century they began to degenerate into poor white trash. Their women had become loose and promiscuous and the men violent, racist, drunken Ku Klux Klanners. They still lived in a big, gray plantation house on a hill. Their only claim to their lost dignity was that the old man was the justice of the peace. There were three boys, and all of them had hot tempers—violent, hot tempers. The youngest one had had an argument with Lindsey in front of J. C. Himes's shop. Lindsey cussed him out and went on home, walking with his dogs. The boy got in his pickup truck and ran him down and killed him. Gadge was there, and didn't defend his brother against a white man.

When Lindsey died he suddenly became a town hero and martyr—when he was alive he was an illiterate black man who could play the guitar and could hunt and tell jokes and was loved by dogs. He talked to them like people. He was loved by women—whom he sometimes talked to like dogs. He was the leader of a band of local degenerates like himself. After his death the miscreants became "reborn" Christians. Uncle Gadge wrote a play about his death. He made it seem like his brother, in a manner of speaking, was a rural Jesus Christ, because so many people got religion after he died.

From where I sat on the bed I could see the poster from my uncle's play. The words "Black Christ" were written in big, thick, black letters over the picture of a black man carrying a cross into a sunset. It was very symbolic. In the background were many farmers with their heads dropped in mourning for this pastoral Christ. Then these words: ". . . The hero was kind . . . Christian . . ." —*Time* magazine.

Lindsey wasn't Christian. He was black, and angry, and young, and wanting to live. He was a nappy-headed nigger who couldn't read and write and he hated white people for what they did to him. That's what made me tremble every time I thought of him. Uncle Gadge "whitenized" him.

The problem I was having then in my personal life was trying to come to terms with the hypocrisy of the Black Bourgeoisie. I was so antimaterialistic that it hurt me to see my uncle driving a 450SL Mercedes, knowing how he never had sent a tombstone to put on his own brother's grave. You take, for instance, their attitude about almost anything.

Boy, talking about being corny and unhappy! Or take any of their famous black show-biz friends. Talk about uneducated, retarded millionaires! How they envy white people! But you would never know that if you were white! Aunt Lottie serves assiduously on the committee of the Sugar Ray Robinson Youth Foundation; each year, the Neiman-Marcus fortnight demands her presence; around April she gotta rush off to the Viennese Culture Club's Opera Ball, or in May she has to be at the annual five-star benefit held by the Los Angeles Philharmonic Orchestra.

As the chairperson of the local chapter of Afri-Care she has helped send thousands of dollars to Somalia to help feed our starving African brothers, but she wouldn't help any black person down the street in the ghetto who really needed money to buy groceries. They were both outraged about the Atlanta tragedy and no doubt sent money there, too. To soothe their guilty conscience they would send money anywhere to help blacks as long as they could be assured the blacks would do their suffering somewhere off in Georgia or across the ocean.

What's wrong with that, you ask. Nothing if you're white and half dead: but she's black and ain't that rich, and pretends to be richer than she really is. But Aunt Lottie never knew what we had to suffer to produce my uncle even if he was going through culture shock in Hollywood. And we had produced him. He had come from our own particular family, and who's to say that if Lindsey had not been killed Gadge would've ever written a play or would've ever made it to Hollywood, or ever married a doctor's daughter and been able to send his son to *est*, where he stood in front of these people and said, "I hate being black!" at age twelve.

My mind was a blue reverie. Who was I? Why did I do comedy? I was a motherfucker fighting a lot of self-doubt about my art, yet I knew if I didn't do it I would die, I would be just another statistic, another nobody, a very frightening proposition. Performing was a way of explaining to others what had happened to me in the South. It helped give the chaotic injustice of the White Man's World some order, some justice, some meaning, and, perhaps, some dignity.

Maybe Buddy was right about that existential comedy. The need to make the white goddamn world my stage is what I'd like to satisfy, boy. I mean, just get up there and tell the whole world to kiss my ass! *Lord Kiss My Arse!*

Now if I'd did a scene like that on the stage, Thalia would've come at me with a knife. *You can't do that, it's too racist!* Why is it racist? *Just because you're offending black people!* No, I'm not, I'm not offending anybody, I'm just telling what actually happened, and what actually happened *is* funny. Can't I have some fun too! Why must we always serve the bourgeoisie (like Buddy said). Look at Billy Badman's life . . . Isn't that what Billy Badman's comedy teaches us? Isn't that the great lesson of the century? *Oh, Jonah, you're bitter!* Yeah, yeah, and who in the fuck ain't bitter. *But it's not funny!* It is funny, I ought to know, I tell stuff like this to my friends and they laugh! (I see myself talking to Buddy and Fatso.) *They're laughing at you, not with you!* How would you know, you're a dried-up Jewish cunt! *How dare you speak to me like that, you'll never work in Hollywood again. Never, never, never again!* (A new musical number?) And you know what?—I don't give a fuck! Except I do. Which is why this little scene only takes place in my head! Sometimes, if not all the time, I laugh at myself thinking what would happen if Thalia knew what was really going on in my head when I walked onto that stage. If only I could tell the audience what I *really* thought and didn't have to stand up there and tell the jokes while they, piss-drunk, laugh at me like I'm some goddamn clown! And on top of that, I stand up there and tell the same jokes night after night, week after week, month after month, year after year, and all I get is some measly applause. You know what they can do with their applauses? YOU guessed it—and I'll tell you something else, too; getting laid out of the Comedy Club ain't no big goddamn deal—not the big deal it's cracked up to be. I can't even begin to explain to my comedian friends how unhappy I am, how I live in this shell where I hold back all of my true fucking feelings about myself, about them, about the Comedy City Club. These guys—good comics that they are —don't even *think* the way I do. For them the stage is only a way of making it on the *Tonight* show and the *Tonight* show is only a way of making it on some sit-com and the sit-com is only a way of making a couple hundred grand a year which for them is a feasible plan. But me? Fuck, I couldn't even dream that way, those are white dreams. The world is already graced with one Bill Cosby. I'm not into that shit. What I want to use the stage for is to express myself. "Express myself." Big words, my friend. Yes, I know, but it's what I want to do. I want to yell out everything that's inside me. Why is it they only allow Billy Badman to do that? Huh? I ask you, ladies and gentlemen. Why only one of us can do that? Why is it that this guy passing the coke to me right now doesn't even know what I'm capable of doing as a comic—"Jonah, man, you just keep telling them jokes about the Preacher and the Deacon's Wife and you'll be another Flip Wilson"—doesn't know and doesn't care.

# 4

AUNT Lottie was on the phone. She has these girlfriends that she has to call every morning to dish dirt about everybody else in Hollywood.

"Did you see the cover of *Jet!*" she said. "Sidney Poitier is on the cover of *Jet* with a white woman? Girl, you ain't seen that?"

My Aunt Lottie. She is a great person. She joins all the right clubs—but she's a member of the Zwanza Club, which is this organization of all the black women in show business. Each year they throw an annual ball where all the black celebrities come with their wives and dance. Think of a black Rotary club and you'll be close. This last year, they invited Sidney Poitier to be the featured guest. Not until Sidney Poitier had accepted the honor did the members of the Zwanza Club realize that he was married to a white woman and this caused considerable problems with the members of that club, and to show just how liberal they are, they all pretended that it didn't matter. You should've seen the way the black women acted when Sidney Poitier walked in with his white wife. "Oh, how are you, Mrs. Poitier?" "Oh, Mrs. Poitier, you really look divine." "Oh, Mrs. Poitier, how are your children?"

But as soon as they were out of earshot they talked about her like a dog. "Honey, did you see that bitch? And did you see how she got all red in the face when a black woman even got near him? Ooooohhh, hhush! She just scared he gonna leave her for a black woman!" "Well, you know I've always said he shouldn't have left that black woman and their four kids for that white bitch!" *"He has four black children!"* "Yes, he do!" "Lord, how mercy!" "And what about his picture with her on the cover of *Jet?*"

I sat down at the table before the steak, which I wouldn't eat, and which I had asked not to be cooked for me, and poured myself some coffee.

Though I repeatedly told her that I was a vegetarian, Aunt Lottie, a strong-willed Christian, still cooked the steak and placed it before my chair on the table. I liked a lot of brown rice, the true diet of an enterprising clown, but Aunt Lottie didn't believe me. I liked it when people believed me.

She was going on and on about Sidney Poitier and "that white woman." I was tempted to yell to her in the other room: "That ain't no white woman—that's his wife!" lest she forget, but instead I leaned over the table.

Uncle Gadge turned to me and said in a voice I'd expect from my father: "Your aunt and I—well, we've been talking about your future. We think it's about time you found yourself another place to live."

"Sure," I agreed. What was funny was, he just didn't know how much I agreed. Man, did I want to split that scene! After you've witnessed a million of Lottie's Praise the Lords and Gadge's unfaithfulness, you're ready to get out of there. At least I was.

After dinner, I went to my room and began my daily exercises of fifty sit-ups, twenty push-ups. After the exercise I stood in front of my full-length mirror, and practiced a monologue.

When I was a kid I answered an ad in the back of a comic book that promised to teach me magic. My father used to amuse me by the curious childlike look he gave me when I made a cigarette disappear, or changed a green silk handkerchief into a red one, or produced flowers from a brown paper sack, or took a quarter and made it vanish through my ears with sure and consummate skill. I had amazed him with one of my pocket tricks; he would follow the movement of my hands out of the corner of his eye, all the time pretending that he wasn't looking, and then he'd say something like, "I ain't got time for that foolishness, boy," or "You can't fool me, I use to do that same trick when I was a boy, and I done forgot more tricks than you'll ever learn. Take that cigarette out of your sleeve before it burn the devil out of you!" When I showed him that it wasn't up my sleeve, he would come back with something like: "Uh-huh, you slick little devil, don't bother me with that foolishness!" And then sipping black coffee off his saucer, he would turn to my mother and pretend that he was angry. "Woman, I done told you about letting him read all them crazy books! It done ruint his eyes, next thing you know he gonna be prancing around here like Oscar Lee, and then we will have two sissies in the family!" My father was a typical hypocrite so when he wanted to impress one of his friends he would send for me. "Give him that cigarette," he'd say to his friend. After I'd make the cigarette disappear to the amazement of all who had eyes, he'd chuckle with pride and say, "What did I tell you? That boy's going to college!"

Now, working out alone in front of the mirror, I learned the art of appearing spontaneous about even the most deliberate effect. It was as good as practicing before the Hollywood Wits, I thought. I took a break, smoked a cigarette, and decided to do a new monologue for my "Southern Stories" section. When I was about fourteen I had discovered racism in television. My family had the first television in the community. Everybody came to our house to watch it. Somehow my grandmother, Gramma Connie, led us to believe that only if you were white and rich could you be on television. We decided that we would audition for the local talent contest in Wilmington. Gramma Connie would be watching the talent show, and there we'd be. Wouldn't that be enough to amaze any grandmother?

To get to the audition in Wilmington, thirty miles away, we had to take a train. Early that Saturday morning, Buck and I set out with our bag of tricks and the hula hoop.

In addition to producing a goldfish in an empty glass of water, producing coins out of thin air and making dollar bills disappear into even thinner air, reading minds, making predictions, pulling a live possum out of a stovepipe, I had prepared a special number for the talent show—levitation. In this act, I hypnotized Buck, raised him about three feet off the ground and passed a hula hoop over him to demonstrate to all skeptics that there were, in the most literal sense, no strings attached.

Planning my conquest of the local talent show, I had worked on my magic act for weeks. Instinctively, I knew about the racial barriers to young colored magicians, but I was intent on throwing them a bag of tricks that they had never, in their wildest fantasies, imagined. What I guess I was betting on was that the racists would be so fascinated by the tricks that I was performing—a goldfish suddenly appearing in an otherwise empty glass of water—that they would not notice that I was black. Had I then known the improbability of such a miracle, I could not have been driven with such self-assurance, confidence, skill, and talent; for the real illusion, the great trick of life, was: *to beat the enemy at his own game, but only on your terms!*

The fact that I didn't believe in my tricks but that others did—this was my ace in the hole.

That morning Buck and I stood on the train track waiting for the nine-thirty express.

Nobody had stopped the train in years.

The sun was already hot, and Buck was sweating from his forehead and nose.

"Careful," I cautioned.

Buck was so scared on the train that I had to tell him stories. He was scared of the white people all staring at us. So I told him stories about our ancestors, throwing in a bawdy joke or two.

On my mother's side, the Waddell side of the family, from which Charles Waddell, the famous black writer, descended, who had written stories for *The Atlantic Monthly* for ten years until they discovered he was black—from this side of the family comes magic mixed with the real. One of these women was notorious because she was extremely beautiful. She was very young, she had had a batch of children, one of which had in turn had a batch of children also; anyway, it turned out that when she was only thirty-five she was approached by one of her grandchildren, a young handsome man, who had been instructed by his father that he should go out into the world and find himself a woman. The young boy went out across the fields and fell in love with his grandmother. He didn't know any more about what was happening to him than Oedipus did. All he knew was that he looked into a house and saw the most beautiful woman in the world. Later, when he told his father about the woman, his father simply said, "Great. Wonder who that could be?" But later, when the identity of the affair was established, the father said, "Crazy nigger! You fucked my mother!" All the son could do was leave home before his father killed him, which the father promised to do to him. To which the son replied: "So what, you fucked my mother." But the grandmother had known that her lover was the issue of her own loins, as all women know the identity of their love is always either their son or their father. She hadn't said anything until the boy had burst inside her like an exploding sunflower. When the grandson had rolled over, she said, "You naughty child! Come back here and hit it a few more strokes, and then get up and get me a switch!"

Then I told him the one about Nicodemus and Christ, as told to me by my father. Christ was a black magician who shocked the white world with his tricks. Nicodemus was a skeptical man. He climbed up to the top of a tree to see Christ coming along the road. Christ, a dark-skinned man, with a razor cut along the side of his right cheek, had a shiny gold tooth in his mouth, where he had had one of his teeth knocked out in a fight over some whore. Christ had been billed as the greatest magician in sandals, but Nicodemus was still skeptical. As Christ was coming along with the multitude behind him, he turned and threw his finger at Nicodemus up in the treetop and said, "Nicodemus, I will be with thee for dinner."

Nicodemus was a skeptical man, and a skeptical man is the type who if you lay a pile of hot shit in front of his nose will say something like, "No, I don't smell nothing. Smell like a flower to me." If you tell him that life is short, his answer is, "Life is anything but short, my friend. Fact is, life is too long." If he owes you money he will deny it on the pretext that he doesn't believe it, as if his debt to you was a philosophical question. When his wife has his child, he looks at it and says, "Hmm! Wonder who his daddy is!" When people he is supposed to love die, he says, "Another day, another dollar."

When he is walking with you at nighttime, he talks of nothing but daytime. When he is going to the town, he says that he is going to the city. When his children are still hungry after dinner, he makes them go to bed! "They too young to know anything about hungry. Go to bed!"

When Christ told Nicodemus "I will be with thee for dinner," Nicodemus was so shocked that he slipped all the way down the tree, causing all the bark to fall from the tree, and this is why sycamore trees never have any bark on them right to this day.

When Nicodemus got home he told his wife, "Jesus Christ

is coming to dinner. But we gonna fix his ass. He suppose to know everything. He suppose to be another Father Divine, but I'm gonna Father Divine his ass. Go out there and put that baby under the washpot. He suppose to be able to see through things. I want you to put that baby under the washpot, and I'm gonna see if he is the man he is suppose to be!"

When Christ got to the door, Nicodemus told him, "Come out to the back yard, Christ, got something I want to show you." When they got to the back door, Nicodemus said, "See that washpot over there? What's under it?"

Christ looked at Nicodemus. Nicodemus was a Jew, see. He was real skeptical. And this story is supposed to explain why Jews don't eat pork.

"What's under the washpot."

Christ was mad. He paused, stroking his beard.

Finally he looked up at Nicodemus and said, "A pig."

Nicodemus fell out laughing, because he had caught Christ. He glanced over at his wife and everybody was laughing at Christ.

"Turn the washpot over, honey," Nicodemus said, after he had had a good laugh.

The wife turned the washpot over, to show Christ the baby. But just as she picked the washpot up, something ran from under it like a wild animal. When Nicodemus saw that it was a pig, he almost croaked. Christ looked at him and said in his sassy, slick voice, "What's cooking for dinner?" That's why Jews don't eat pork.

The train put us off around ten-thirty. The goldfish was dead. We went to the five-and-dime and purchased another one. There was a civil rights sit-in going on in the coffeeshop there and we got sidetracked a little, watching that. We got to the audition just in time.

The white man who served as the MC sat back and watched us do our tricks, his cigar cocked to the side of his head, and he was just as skeptical as Nicodemus. Me and

Buck performed like champs. All of the tricks worked beautifully. Every time I finished a trick you could hear the white girls getting excited. After we finished, the man said that it was fine, just great, that he'd call us and let us know.

Just before we left he looked down at me and snickered, "You niggers know how to do a disappearing act?"

After we were outside, Buck was mad. We got to the train station, and Buck was still mad. I didn't know what to say to him. And then finally he said, "Man, I didn't want to be on the motherfucker anyway."

"Me, neither."

"I just wanted to see if they would let us on the motherfucker."

"Me, too."

"But, you know, we could have been on it if we wanted to. I didn't want to be on it that bad. What about you?"

"No, I just wanted to see if we COULD be on it."

"We were ALMOST on it."

"I know it."

"But we fooled them, didn't we? I mean, we fooled the shit out of them. They thought we were real magicians, man, that cracker's eyes got big as the moon when you produced goldfish! And then we did the one with the cigarette! That was fun, watching them crackers with their mouths hanging open!"

"We were almost on it, though."

"That's BETTER than being on it, man!"

When we got home we were so excited that we told everybody that we were going to be on television—almost. Everybody was so excited that they didn't mind the "almost." That Saturday night, everybody showed up to see us on television, but me and Buck talked so much about *almost* being on it (I did the same tricks that I did for the white man, so that everybody could get an idea of what actually happened) that our absence from the TV screen was hardly noticed. Like

Buck said, "Sometimes *almost* is enough." Even Gramma Connie went around saying, "You know them two boys were *almost* on television." She was so proud.

When I woke up—for I'd fallen asleep after my exercises —it was morning and I smelled bacon in the kitchen.

# 5

"YOU'LL like this job," Uncle Gadge said. We had been driving about half an hour without exchanging one word. He pulled up in front of a gray-looking building off Washington Street and parked in front of a faded, plantation-type house.

"What is this?" I asked, looking at the dilapidated buildings that lined the street.

"This is where I work," he replied.

"I thought you worked for a film studio," I said.

"I do—this is it," he said. We got out of the car and walked to the plantation house.

"Why does it look like a plantation house?" I asked him.

"Used to be the old Goldwyn studios," he said. "This was the Tara plantation in *Gone with the Wind.*"

It had been Democracy Studio in 1919. It was a one-room deal. Democracy Studio in 1935—they built the façade that was in *Gone with the Wind.* In the lobby there were some aerial photos. From the airplane's view it looked like a small sugar plantation. A water tank with the letters DEMOCRACY stood high over the stage building and the tall Ivory Tower. You could see the hospital and the lumber building and the prop building and farther to the upper left the river running through it. The studio looked like a small town. In a way, it was. The difference being that a little town might produce sugar, but this little town produced film.

On the opposite side of the lobby was a press-book cover for Oscar Micheaux's *Harlem after Midnight* (1935). The light-skinned sisters had their big legs stuck out in a mock satire of a Ziegfeld Follies chorus line, their satin-toed dance shoes pointing to the caption "An epidemic of high-yallers and sugar-cured browns straight from Harlem and sizzlin' hot! Yeah man!" On each side of the girls, as the crude hand of the lithograph strove for balance, were pitches like, "In a story that is different! Melodrama with music!" and "Gangdom in action again—but from a new angle—the angle of the kidnapper!"

No doubt about it—that was a different angle.

Another poster boasted an Oscar Micheaux "Great Colored Cast Production in TEMPTATION, featuring Lorenzo Tucker (better known as 'Dark Cable') and Slick Chester."

What kind of studio was this, anyway? Some kind of all-black production company?

I was turned over to an old man who'd been with Democracy since it was a silent-movie studio. His name was Terry Reese, and he took me to the mailroom and showed me what my duties were.

"Is there much prejudice here?" I asked. A white man was walking with us.

"Prejudice?" Mr. Terry Reese stopped and looked at me. "Nah, suh, cain't say there's any here." Then he waved to the buildings. "This is a studio—a film studio in California. Lak Mistuh Jack Valenti sez yesditty on TeeVee, when he made dat speech to the END-DOUBLE-AYE-SEE-PEA?"

"The NAACP?" I asked.

"Yes"—he grinned—"that's it. Didya catch it?"

"No, I didn't," I said. "How was it? Better than *Roots?*"

"Oh, yes. It was sumpin'—he sez dat the business ain't interested in none of dis here racial equality—here, it's jus' turnin' a buck! Boy, and dat END-DOUBLE-AYE-SEE-PEA jes' had to sit back and take it! Mister Valenti, chairman of the Motion Picture Association of America, he's whup it on 'em! He-he-he!" He laughed. And then, after we'd walked a bit, he added: "Pig know which tree to rub against. This is the best of all possible worlds for the black people."

I didn't have enough experience to doubt him. "I see," I said—I did, too. I really did. It wasn't easy, though, I can tell you that. In the first place, you could hardly hear the words. He muttered everything. On top of that, he spoke in these riddles, the meanings of which were clear only to himself, and then he'd laugh at his own self as if he'd said the funniest joke in the world. When the white man walking beside us turned off into the projection building, Mr. Reese said to me: "So your uncle got you this job, huh?"

"Yes, but didn't he say anything to you about an acting job?" I asked.

"No, why?"

"Well, because I am a comedian. I was sort of looking for a start. My Uncle Gadge knows I've been busting my ass trying to get in a film. I just thought that by some act of mercy he'd considered me for a part in one of these films he writes."

"Are you complaining?" he asked as he pulled the door of a building open, and another white man came out. "Better gravy dan no grease a'tall," he said, and bowed to the white man with the tip of his head. "Morning, suh." He grinned.

The man went on his way. I couldn't understand why Mr. Reese spoke in a dialect whenever a white man came close to us but when we were walking along just before entering the building, he spoke to me in plain English. Why did he switch to speaking Negro dialect whenever some white person was present?

We came to the swiveling doors of a glass building. Entering behind him, I saw people sitting at a lunch counter. A lady wearing a Marie Antoinette dress was having the Onion Soup Special.

"Dat dere—dat's the commissary," Mr. Reese said, and

gave his little "House Nigger" chuckle—the meaning of which I'm still not too clear about. And then he added one of his little proverbs: "Meller muskmelon hollers at you frum de fence, sho!"

We went downstairs, past the lavatories, to his little office. "Sit down," he told me. "If you ever need to find me, I'm here." He opened his arms in a gesture to mean the room—to look at it.

I looked at it—it was where the dude slept! It had a cot, a little night table with a private phone, radio, and so on.

"Now what was this about acting? You thought you were going to get an acting job?" Mr. Reese lit a cigarette, and took a drag. "There are a hundred white boys who'd like to have your position—not to say nothin' about the minorities . . . So consider yourself lucky. Like Jack Valenti says, this is the best place for the advancement of the black people! The best of all worlds."

"Oh, I consider myself lucky," I said.

"You'd better," he snapped.

"Say, Mr. Reese," I began timidly, "why do you speak dialect when white people are around and normal English with me?"

"Oh—you noticed that? Ha! It's just another side of my talented personality." He laughed. "I'm talented like George Kirby. I can do anybody's voice."

"Oh, I see," I said—surprised at his answer. "But does a servile attitude come with it?" I asked.

"Oh, you don't understand," he said. "White folks feel comfortable when I talk like dat. When I add proverbs to my speech, they find it colorful. It improves my acting ability, and it don' hurt nobody!" he said, falling comically into dialect. "You know," he joked, "da pig dat runs off wid da ear er corn gits little mo dan de cob."

"Talking in proverbs—is that what you have to do to succeed around here?" I asked, seeing as I was going to have a pretty rough time of it—since I didn't know too many proverbs.

"It helps," he said.

"Then I'm fucked—and a long ways from home!" I exclaimed.

He shook his head encouragingly. "Dat ain't bad—that ain't bad at all!" He laughed, then got up. "Come on and I'll show you your duties."

I had to sort out the mail and make deliveries to the script department, studio, the executive tower, the writers' building, the producers' building, the casting building, out to the bungalows, and sometimes the back lot. I also sorted the fan mail for the movie stars. On Thursdays I got to drive Mr. Grayeye's Rolls to do his errands.

One good thing about this job, though, was that nobody saw you. They looked at you but they didn't see you. You were invisible to them. I felt like Perseus with his Cap of Darkness stolen from the Graeae that gave him invisibility so he could elude the Gorgons. I was just the mailboy. I could listen to important decisions being made—something impossible for writers, producers, or actors. I could talk to the chairman of the board as well as the lowliest employees.

"Now, my boy, how would you like to see how we actually make a film?" Mr. Reese asked me.

"Fine," I answered.

"Come with me," he said, and we crossed the room and opened a closet. "There is just one more thing I must tell you about your duties. The man who you are replacing is no longer with us."

"What happened to him?"

"He died—suddenly—in the middle of a sentence—he dropped dead." He took a jacket out of the closet. "But that's no matter of yours! Here, take his jacket and wear it until we can get you one. You're required to wear this uniform while you're working here as a messenger."

He gave me the jacket, and I put it on.

"How does it fit?" he asked.

It fitted me perfectly. "Nice," I told him, and he gave me a strange look.

"You're exactly Major's size," he commented. "Look a little like him, too."

We entered the studio. They were videotaping a religious show called *The Elma Gantry Hour*.

There was a live audience, and I could see it both on the television monitors and live on the stage.

From behind the hot lights of the camera, a stocky man with a toupee, wiping the sweat from his soft, feminine face, slammed his open palm on the face of the crippled, gray lady: "HAVE YOUUUUUUU BEENNNNNNN TOUCHED BY GAWD TODAYY?"

I knew that he was going to heal her of her crippledness but I could see now that he was just a fat guy with a scheme. On the TV monitor we see him perform the miracle.

"DO YOU BELIEVE THE LORD JESUS CHRIST CAN HEAL YOU TODAY?"

But I can see right now that his toupee has moved off and I can see now the edge of makeup that divides his face from his red neck.

"HEAL THIS WOMAN, LORD!"

Slapping the old believer upside the head with such a powerful lick, the woman falls back in her wheelchair. On the TV monitor it looked real. I can see that he has hit her so hard some don't know if she's healed or not.

"ARE YOU HEALED? HAS THE LORD HEALED YOU? JUST SPEAK UP CLOSER TO THE MIKE . . . DON'T BE AFRAID . . . HE-HE-HE . . . IT WOULDN'T BITE YA. I SAY, DID THE LORD HEAL YOU? . . ."

Stunned, embarrassed, her head bleeding from the blow, the crippled lady said, "I . . . I . . . uh . . ."

"THANK GOD FOR THAT! DIDYA HEAR WHAT SHE SAID?" Pushing the mike back into her face, he knows she cannot lie before the almighty air waves.

"YES—"

"NOW, WALK, WALK, WALK FOR US!"

The lady attempts to walk. She goes a few steps and collapses.

On the monitor it looked like she walked a few steps before we cut to the close-up of Reverend Gantry's face, but I can plainly see now that she's fallen down.

"Are we still on the air?" the reverend asks.

"No," the assistant producer answers.

"Well, get this goddamn lady outta here," the reverend tells him. "I don't want to see any cripples today," he said, wiping his brow. "Just bring in the asthma victims. NO DAMN CRIPPLES AND BLIND PEOPLE PLEASE!"

We walked into sound stage 32 and I saw a black man stripped to his waist and a white man flogging him with a whip.

"Action!" the director called.

"Quiet on the set!"

The white man started beating the devil out of the brother. I was so shocked that I wanted to run in and stop them, but when I saw the Panavision camera tracking in on the scene I realized that it was just a movie.

"That's a Simon Legree scene from *Uncle Tom's Cabin*," Mr. Reese explained. "We doin' a remake of the Universal one in 1935."

We got on a motor-truck and drove out to the back lot. I saw a long line of slaves on the auction block—black actors playing slaves, but what's the difference.

"What's that?" I asked.

"This is the auction scene from *Gone with the Wind*," he

explained. "Mr. Grayeye the Third has seen *Gone with the Wind* 350 times."

"Is this a remake, too?"

"Oh, yeah. We specializes in remakes," he said, grinning like a house nigger himself.

When we came back into sound stage 32 he showed me three lavish sets for the remake of *Green Pastures* (1936). A couple black sissies in long wings flew by. I guess they were Angel Gabriel and his buddy. Then he showed me the set for the remake of *Stormy Weather* (1943). A Cab Calloway look alike dressed in a zoot suit and a big white hat and white shoes danced down stairways while an orchestra played "The Jumpin' Jive." In yet another set, a remake of Al Jolson's *Everybody Sing* (1937), a white man in blackface was singing "Goin' to Heaven on a Mule," while little white actors (boys) in blackface played Bakelite harps under Styrofoam gum trees at the top of which a Plexiglas possum sat. But the most lavish of all was the set for *Rhapsody in Black and Blue* (1931). Mr. Reese pointed out that the whole band was supposed to look like they were playing music on a cloud in heaven—and it did too. Some of the actors—all of them black—were stripped down to the waist, with leopard skins thrown across their shoulders, striding around playing long trumpets. Another one was the king, because they had him sitting up in this throne with a big awkward-looking drum major's hat on and old epaulettes on his shoulders and a king-size grin on his chops. Next to him was a light-skinned sister giving you much fleshy thigh. Some naked girls were dancing around them. A short, chubby man with a face like Peter Lorre and dressed like Rhett Butler came up to us.

"Hello, Terry," he said; then, looking at me: "Who's this?"

"Dis is Gadge's nephew," Mr. Reese explained.

"Oh, yes," the fat man said. "I'm Mr. Mortimer Grayeye." He took a cigar out of his mouth. "I run this studio. So you're going to be with us for a while?"

"Yes," I answered.

"Is this set wonderful? I'm doing a remake of all the old black classics, including *Cabin in the Sky* and *Star Spangled Rhythm*—very underrated pictures. That's the comedy division. Under the dramatic division I am doing all remakes of *Roots*-like pictures. I'm doing your race a big favor."

"That's nice," I said—it was nice, too. Just think of him going to all that trouble for us.

"I'm doing a remake of Herb Jeffries as the first black cowboy with his sidekick Manton Moreland. Remember those?"

"Yes," I said. I wonder why when a white person discovers something about black culture that's a million years old he always assumes every black person should congratulate him on his new knowledge.

"Oh, yes, I remember," I lied.

Mr. Mortimer Grayeye the Third winked at me and patted me on the shoulder. "You're a good kid, Jonah. Do you think you can fill Major's shoes?"

"I'll try."

"That's the spirit," he said.

In his black riding pants and black leather riding boots and his beret and thin Clark Gable moustache, Mr. Grayeye was congeniality itself. Taking out his personal Maurice's Snack 'N Chat menu from the leather pouch of his producer's chair, he ordered, "I'll have the link sausages, grits, black-eyed peas, a side order of yams, a glass of Maurice's special sauce, and a potato pie."

"Shall he take the car?" Mr. Reese asked.

"Yes, let him take the car. Okay," Mr. Grayeye the Third said. "We'll see how you do with this. Major could do it in an hour. It's ten-thirty now."

I felt obliged to tell him how much I appreciated the opportunity to work for him. "I like it here," I said.

"Good. Our philosophy here is simple: Art is the reproduction of reality with feelings. That's why we make remakes here. I like to follow Aristotle's principle about art, and it hasn't failed me yet. Sonny, do you know the two books that have influenced my life? Aristotle's *Art of Poetry* and Harriet Beecher Stowe's *Uncle Tom's Cabin*."

"I'm familiar with both of them," I told him.

"Good. Read them well and one day I'll make you a director. See you later."

"He-he-he! Don't it jes' tear you up to see a man dat smart?" Terry Reese commented as we moved along.

Back in his office, Mr. Reese gave me the car keys. "When you get there, go in the back and ask for Mabel. You sho' you got everything down he said he wanted?" he asked. "He funny about what he eat."

I assured him I did and went out. The car was a two-tone gray-and-maroon Rolls-Royce that Mr. Reese told me Major used for special errands for Mr. Grayeye the Third. I jumped in and headed for Maurice's Snack 'N Chat on Pico. As I drove through the traffic on La Cienega I thought about that Mortimer Grayeye the Third and the Democracy Studio. Wasn't that a trip?

# 6

MAURICE'S Snack 'N Chat sat in the middle of a teeming street in the ghetto. A young black girl in a purple jumpsuit and a yellow blond wig leaned from the corner into the window of a long lavendar Cadillac Seville. An irate bus pulled up behind the Seville, and the driver honked his horn annoyingly; two young dudes slipped between the bus and the Seville seconds before the bus rammed into the Seville, though they never stopped talking. The door of the Seville popped open and its driver jumped to the street. The bus driver leaned out the window and screamed at him—said he could get the hell out of his way. Gold chains flashed around the Cad driver's neck and wrists and in his mouth there was gold when he snarled—all picking up and glittering in the sunlight. Just then the police car showed up, just in time to hear the bus driver yell, "Who the hell you think you are—blocking up the damn street!"

"You cocksucker! You hit my car!" the Seville driver yelled back.

"Fuck you and your car, nigger! I got a Seville, too!"

"Get out the bus, motherfucker," the pimp said, and quickly took off his coat. He had on a light blue shirt. "Get off the bus!" He folded his coat neatly and placed it on the trunk of the Seville.

"Get out of my way, before I run over you, you damn fool!" yelled the bus driver.

The cops' car turned around; the pimp pushed back a few

people, knocking one lady down, as he ran to the front of the bus and dragged the driver out and started to beat him in the face.

The young black sister in the purple jumpsuit started hitting the driver across the head with her purse, which was of considerable size. Passengers stood by waiting as if they were viewing it on television. When the driver tried to defend himself, either the pimp or his whore would hold him while the other one took advantage of the opportunity. You could tell the pimp and the whore knew how to work together. They beat him as if they were trying to say something tender to each other.

Finally the cops came up to them, apparently taking their time. They broke up the fight—what little of it was left by then. Then they asked people what happened, but none of the bystanders said they saw what happened.

"Officer," the pimp was saying, "he deliberately ran into my car!"

"Be quiet until we get to you!" the cop with the notebook said to him.

"Say, mister . . ." I heard a woman's voice calling. I turned. There was this good-looking sister about my age signalling to me to come over to where she was. Where she was, was on the corner. I'd just parked the car and was standing by the meter. She was standing sorta near the wall. Between me and her were the people in cars, slowing down and staring at the police, the pimp, and the bus driver across the street.

"Say, brother. . . ."

I went over to her. Close up, she was really young . . . and juicy, too. She looked like Lena Horne in *Stormy Weather* when she sang the title song. Except in this case, it wasn't a storm, but a lot of ghetto noise and people carrying on. A big slit tore up the side of her red skirt revealed caramel-colored thighs, and when I got close enough her breasts looked like two big, ripe cantaloupes.

"You wanna catch some action?" she asked.

"Yeah, I wanna catch some action," I said. I did, too. Really—I did!

". . . How much you got?"

"How much *what* I got?"

"Say, country boy . . . money . . . ain't you hip?"

"Yeah, I'm hip . . ."

I stuck my hands into my pocket. I didn't have much. I knew that even before I drew out the two twenties.

". . . Hey," I said, about to hand it over to her when somebody grabbed me by the arm and spun me around.

"So . . . you the new replacement for Major, eh?"

I was face to face with a thug about six feet tall. All I could see was that his face was beat in. He had a gray bowler hat, and had a couple guys with him.

He turned to the girl. "Beat it, bitch," and the girl took off. She didn't even take the money.

"Say, you forgot the money," I shouted at her. She looked at me like I was really stupid. Then I thought of a nice thing to say. "How're you going to buy your school books without the money?" She gave me another double take, and strutted off, and no doubt a better person for it, too.

"Don't try to be smart, motherfucker," the guy said, and grabbed me by the arm.

I snatched my arm out of his grip and took off. After losing them in the crowd, I started to thinking about what happened. Major must've been doing some extra business on the side, I thought, using Mr. Grayeye's expensive status symbol as a means of impressing some thugs. What else but that two-toned Rolls-Royce could make them think I was somehow connected to Major.

I finally made it to Maurice's Snack 'N Chat.

I went to the back and asked for Mabel and this big fat older sister nodded her head slowly as I explained what my boss wanted.

"What yuh name is, chile?" she asked finally, and I told her.

"Come here, Piggy," she called out, and this old fat man came out. "Look here at this new one. Major died and now they send this 'un."

The man looked at me.

"He-he-he!" he cackled.

"I hope I meet your approval," I said.

They both ignored me and looked at me and laughed. I didn't have any idea of what they were laughing about. I'd 've felt embarrassed had I not been a Southerner myself and wasn't familiar with the way they acted.

"You come back," Mabel said, glancing up at the clock, "When them two hands are on twelve."

Looking for some way to pass the time, I hit the street. No sooner had I put foot to pavement than I ran into my old friends the thugs again. Reaching out their grabbers for me, they gave chase, but I wasn't about to let them catch me. I ran through the people—knocking them over, upsetting a greengrocery's fruit stand, past the quick-sketch artist, knocking his easel off the sidewalk, on past Uncle Sam's Funeral Home and past the Disco Bar which was right next to it—you can bury your friend and then go next door and have a drink—past the militant dressed in black leather jacket and black beret, standing on the corner of Pico and Catalina—*"Kill whitey!"*—past Reverend Hakeem Abdul Roscoe, minister of money and pastor of the Dare to Be Rich Church of God and Christ—waving from his yellow convertible. His followers called him "Silver Cloud"—GIVE ME YOUR MONEY AND GOD WILL BLESS YOU!—past a hustler with his overcoat opened like a winged bat from which hung a series of Casio watches, Mexican bracelets in various sizes, a collection of diamond rings, an FM/AM cassette recorder, and a Westinghouse toaster—past a pool hall on Pico and Fedora, past another quick-sketcher until I realized it was the same one—I had run in a full circle, ending up where I began— at Catalina and Pico, which is where Maurice's Snack 'N Chat is. Next to it is another place I recognized—Madame X's Fortunes Told Here. If only I could make it that far. I looked behind me. They were still coming at me! "They are coming!" I yelled out loud, but everybody was too busy with their own problems, obsessions, and self-love to even look.

I ducked into the Madame X shop and watched the thugs run by. I peeped outside from my refuge to see what was going on. The thugs had slowed down, sensing that they had lost me. How right they were! But just as I was about to ease out of my secret hiding spot, I saw something I'd imprudently overlooked. One of the thugs had posted himself right in front of Madame X's Fortunes Told Here, and watched in every direction. I couldn't go out there. Just as I was about to move, I heard a voice, presumably coming from the apartment of the root doctor, Madame X. I was standing in the vestibule. As I turned I saw a neon sign in a corner of the room advertising her powers in a brilliant fluorescent glow: SPEND YOUR MONEY WISELY! GET MADAME X TO GIVE YOU THE BEST FORTUNE IN TOWN! ONLY $4.95. SEE JESUS FOR $1.25! SEE ANY PROPHET OF YOUR CHOICE, $.50! SPECIAL RATES ON CHRISTMAS HOLIDAYS!

I turned and looked at the thug again. I couldn't go out there and risk getting killed.

So I turned to the room, peeped in, and saw the root doctor and her client, an old man.

"Well—I come to see Jesus," the old man said. Pushing sixty, he had one of those stingy-brim hats—with that little peacock feather in the side—pushed back on his head exposing a sweat-glistening forehead which reflected the naked light bulb overhead.

"But you ain't gonna see no Jesus for no dollar," Madame X said, pulling a dreadful black shawl up around her enormous body. The man pulled out a dollar and a quarter. Long earrings jangled, mascaraed eyelashes flashed, menacing eyebrows raised, and freshly painted lips almost dripped like blood.

"You ain't gonna see Him for that, either," she told him. "The price for seeing Jesus done gone up again."

"I—I—I didn't know that."

"Well, you know it now. The prices for seeing Jesus went up last week. To see Jesus, you got to pay five-fifty now. You can still see Mary Magdalene for three-fifty, St. Peter for two dollars (she said it like dallors) . . . and you can see the devil fer fifty cents."

The man pulled out some more money and flung it on the table. "I wants to see Jesus—that's all."

"Suit yourself," the root doctor said, gathering up the money. After she did that, I took off.

I laughed all the way back to Maurice's Snack 'N Chat. Fooling around with the fortune-teller, I was already an hour late.

"Where you been, chile?" Mabel asked me in the kitchen.

"Are the orders ready?"

"They been ready. Where you been?"

"Lost," I said. "I got lost."

"Here," Mabel says, shoveling the big brown bag toward me.

"Is it cold?" I asked, suddenly realizing something. Cold soul food don't taste too good.

"You'd be cold, wouldn't you, if you was sitting up for two hours?" Mabel said. "But let me warm it up 'fore you take it."

I waited another ten minutes, then took off for the studio, trying to think up a good excuse. When we worked for whites in the South we had a Set of Excuses, and among them were such items: I could say that some pimp got shot by the cops and his body blocked the traffic for an hour; my cousin came to town and I had to bail him out of jail; some dope addict threw some shit from a building on me and I had to go home and wash up because I didn't want to come to the studio smelling like that. Maybe I could tell him that I nearly got shot by a whore who thought I was her pimp?

As I wheeled the Rolls into the gate, the guard saluted me. I shot over to the set as fast as my legs would carry me. They were in the middle of a scene, but as soon as Mr. Grayeye spied me and the soul food he yelled out, "Cut!"

"You're late," he growled.

"Well, Mr. Grayeye," I said, "the sweet potatoes was just getting off the plane from Georgia. I had to wait until Mabel cooked them."

"These sweet potatoes just came in from Georgia?" he inquired with raised eyebrows, in an incredulous voice so that everybody on the set laughed at me.

"Yes, sir! They fresh as a brand-new baby calf," I said. "You wanna fresh, don'tcha?"

He was too busy scoffing down the soul food to answer. Once I was back in the mailroom, I breathed easy, having gotten out of that narrow scrape.

# 7

BACK in the mailroom later that day, Terry gave me my assignment. I was to take a package over to the writers' building, to Uncle Gadge in Room 203. Before I left, Terry introduced me to my associates in the mailroom.

To get to the writers' building, you had to go way the hell across the lot. They had this really crummy building for the writers. If you were a producer you got a swanky office, and if you were a big star you got a bungalow. But if you were a writer, you got one of these dumps—a cross between a locker and a chicken coop. But Uncle Gadge was practically the biggest writer on the lot so they were always moving him around. Once they had him in the producers' building when he was working on this big TV movie. Now he was back in the writers' building. Usually they put two or three writers in one office, but Uncle Gadge had a whole one to himself. Like I said, to get to the damn thing, you had to go way the hell across the lot. I went over to the wardrobe department and copped one of those motor-trucks to cut down the time.

When I got to the writers' building I parked the thing so nobody could steal it. You'd think that people wouldn't steal on movie lots but you're crazy if you think that because they do. They just swipe things. I mean, they really do! And when you catch them, they always say, they *borrowed* it! I hid it behind these bushes and went inside.

When I got to Uncle Gadge's door, number 203, I

knocked but there was no answer. I thought the secretary had gone to lunch, so I sat in the lobby. Then I heard this moaning coming from his office. I knocked on the door again because I thought he might be in pain or something. Uncle Gadge is not an old guy but he might've had a heart attack or something. Then I heard all this scuffling around in there, and pretty soon this secretary came to the door. She was really young and very good-looking. She cracked the door about an inch. Boy, right away you could see what was going on. Her blouse had been hastily fastened with just one button and she had this silly grin on her mug. She wasn't particularly embarrassed or anything. All she said was, "Oh, it's just Jonah." When I went inside, Uncle Gadge was sitting on the sofa, unbuckled, with his big belly spread out in front of him like a Buddha or something. On the table was some cocaine on a mirror and traces of it was still white on his big, fat brown nose. I was embarrassed as hell and wanted to leave right away, but he kept telling me to stay. I kept saying I had to go somewhere, but he wanted me to stay. He wanted to have a "talk" with me, but what he really wanted me to do was sit there while he made sure I didn't tell Aunt Lottie. He'd never tell you *not* to tell Aunt Lottie. What he'd do, he'd talk you to death so you'd end up telling him what kind of great writer he was. Practically everybody thought so. He'd tell these long-winded stories that made you laugh, and when he'd done that, he figured you'd forgive him for anything else he'd done. Like this secretary, all the time we were sitting there she kept stroking his ego, telling him about how incredible his movies were, while she kept shoveling this cocaine up her snout like a stoker feeding coals in a locomotive engine. I had to sit there for almost two *hours* while he told these stretching lies. Don't ever catch Uncle Gadge snorting cocaine with his secretary. It just spoils your whole afternoon.

The next day I saw an apartment notice on the bulletin board near the punch-in clock. When I got back to the mailroom I called the number and the guy who answered told me about the apartment and it sounded okay. But what really seemed great was that he sounded young and black like me. I took down all the necessary information—his name, the address of the place, and a time that we could meet at—and went back to work.

That day I had to take some mail up to the Ivory Tower, which was this tall, white administration building. I opened a frosted door marked "Minority Film Fund" and went in. A very attractive sister smiled and took the mail. As I turned to leave, I saw Clea Menchan for the first time. She was a tall, blond lady, and I knew that I was going to get to know her well.

That afternoon I found the address of the apartment. As I drove up I saw what it was. It was one of those modern apartment buildings that are so typical of Hollywood in the fifties, with the palm trees with the lights hidden in them that look glamorous at night, and as I came into the courtyard I saw the bikinied, suntanned ladies lying around the swimming pool. I knocked on the door of 107 and this brother came out. He was a big motherfucker, too, but had a nice smile.

He showed me the apartment, which was not a palace or anything, but the rent was cool and I had my own room. But the big plus is that Tull—that was my roommate's name—was the same kind of dude I was—a young, scuffling dude, trying to make it in the white man's world. Tull was a gaffer, the guy that lights the movie sets.

We rapped a bit and smoked a joint and then I told him

I wanted to take the apartment, explaining that sometimes I practiced my comedy out loud and he said he didn't mind. Fact was, he said, he was thinking about being a comic himself, which was funny right there. Anyway, we went down to sign the lease with the manager, who, he told me, was very, very cool.

"Yeah?"

He told me that the manager sold dope to the tenants, that he had a special arrangement with the owner of the building, and that everything was so cool. The manager was a light-skinned black man in his early forties, about five foot eight, who had been an actor, but he had emptied his talent—what little he had—in small parts. "I play doctors," he used to tell me after I'd gotten to know him well. His name was Gussie —Gussie Smith.

When we came in he was sitting behind a desk with a kilo of marijuana and a scale and some plastic bags in front of him. He said he knew it was Tull coming by his footsteps. While Tull told him about me, Gussie fired up one of the joints and we smoked it. I signed the lease, but it would be a week before I could move from my uncle's in Brentwood to the Fountain Lanai on the corner of Sweetzer and Fountain right dab in the heart of West Hollywood.

# 8

DRIVING home from the Fountain Lanai, I wished I
didn't have to spend any more time with my uncle and
aunt. That night, I had to go on at the club, and when I got
home I wanted to practice alone. But when I arrived my
Aunt Lottie was yakking as usual on the phone, managing
to drop all the names in Hollywood. I went to my room, did
a few warm-up exercises, and then stood in front of my mirror and practiced my poses. First, I tried different sports
coats, and then I put a cigarette in my mouth. I couldn't
decide if I should come on smoking or come on with the
cigarette in my inside pocket, and while I'm going into my
opening material, to sort of pull out a cigarette and start
lighting it as casually as hell.

While I was practicing, though, certain thoughts kept running through my head. For some reason I kept thinking of
children. I majored in child care at college, but in Brentwood
you never see really free children. Most of them are as
affected as their parents. They're not really children but
little dwarfs. I had this urge to see some real kids. They leave
such an impression on you, I thought, and that's why I don't
care if an audience don't laugh at me, as long as I leave them
with an impression, the way children always left an impression on me.

Once on a green lawn I saw a pair of naked two-year-old
kids meeting. Barely able to walk, they ran around each
other like little lambs. It made me laugh and cry at the same
time. I felt their innocence and their guilt. I realized that

they had left such a great impression that I was not the same after I walked away.

I would look at my face in the mirror. What did I see? A face intense and tender, angry and serene . . . I thought this is the impression I would like to leave. I decided then that if somebody is going to know me they must know what the tragedy of Lindsey's death signified to me.

I had always wondered why Lindsey's death haunted me. It was certainly not the only one in our family. My uncle Jack's wife killed him in bed on a Sunday morning while he slept. I remember that morning so well then as I did on the day I accompanied my Aunt Amanda and Uncle Lofton to the shanty. Jack and his wife had five children, and they were crying. My brother and I were always playing with them and I remembered them as a big happy family. But I remembered his body still lying with the shotgun wounds on his back. Uncle Lofton let me and my brother see it. I remembered the gentleness of his hands as he led us to the bed, as if we were being taken to visit a distant relative, but we were really first to view the body. A boy, a friend of mine, shot himself in the head one day after school. I'll never forget his name either: Pugh. Pugh Greenlee.

But Lindsey's death was different; he was my uncle. He had been a young man, as I was now. I began to hear the shouting that first brought on that trauma. I stopped and sat on the bed, not able to go on with my practice. "Lindsey is dead!" No, no, no. "THEY killed Lindsey!" Yes, the important thing, I realized, was that he was murdered by a white man. Painful memory, hurt feelings stirred up when I mouthed those words: "Lindsey got killed!"

They said it like it was some kind of disease which you catch if you are a black male living in the South.

Lindsey met every day with my father and their friends under a big shade tree behind my grandmother's house, Gramma Connie. Always wearing a suit and white shirt, and carrying a Bible and pipe, my father would appear and bull-shit with Dick Yoeman. Lindsey and the younger men would come later. They would swap jokes, make fun of each other if there was any pompousness entering into the lean and honest character of country folk. Lindsey would "mock" people in the community. Like African tribal witch doctors, they used humor to dispel the evilness of illusions.

"Good evening, Reverend." Dick Yoeman laughed, making a joke out of my father's religious pretensions but at the same time also respecting it. My father spoke quietly, sat down and loosened his collar, and sat in mute, magnificent silence while Bubble Bland cut him a piece of watermelon. The preacher ate the melon and smacked his lips.

"Gentlemen," he said, "thank the Lord for that."

"You better thank Geeche Gollin," Bubble said. "He the one that stole it."

My father properly ignored the low comment, and took out his pipe. He tapped it on the slate doorstep with a learned and disembodied gesture. He turned his eyes up toward a point in the sky and began to watch the purple edges of a white cloud. This gesture was to indicate to the men that he was going to say something abstract like the clouds above, and that it was something they should all think about. My father was not only a reverend but also a philosopher. People laughed in his face, but respected him behind his back.

"Gentlemen," he said, "I have always wondered: why looking at a woman's behind gives pleasure."

Dick Yoeman's face lighted up and he laughed out loud. "I know the answer to that! The reason why looking at . . ." As he talked, his words dissolved into the air.

He looked at my father, then tried again. "Now doggone it," he said, "that's real simple, Reverend, the reason why—"

Again he failed. The other men watched him make a fool of himself. They watched Dick Yoeman's face change as he suddenly realized that it was one of those philosophical questions. Dick Yoeman had no imagination at all. He had never desired anything beyond what he could put his hands on. His entire life was spent in collecting things, small inconsequential things, like bottles, bugs, pieces of paper. His great love was carving miniature statues of Christ and the saints out of soft pinewood. He carved an entire church, which was supposed to replicate our own church. At a Sunday School convention, he had displayed this entire church. When my father saw the intricate and delicate work, he simply said, "The Bible speaks of people who are gifted with their hands." Dick always attacked my father's questions as if they were pits of knowledge, of facts. His admiration for the reverend's genius was boundless; he only wanted to be able to answer one of his great questions correctly; and his frustration consisted of being baffled by the simplicity of the questions and the complexity of the answers.

In all of these conversations, my father would sit and maintain his position and air of the philosopher. Occasionally, he would slap a mosquito that landed on his black forehead, but always with the exact air of a philosopher.

No one, in fact, could have been as different from each other as my father, and Dick Yoeman.

My father was born in a family with eleven girls and four boys. He had the gift of being proud of human life.

My father was, in his youth, a gambler of any kind of game he could lay hands on. He had met my mother once, but had regarded her with indifference. He had no passion for anything but life; gambling came very easy to him, and he seems to have lived off of what his luck brought him. And then he went to Portsmouth, Virginia, two years after the war and a curious thing happened to him which changed the entire course of his life. He was gambling on the numbers and came almost within one digit of winning ten thousand dollars. The number had been given to him by a woman he'd met, a redbone woman. If he had played the number as she had given it to him, he would have been rich. He changed one digit. He changed a six into a seven. Why had he done that? Up until that time in his life, he cared nothing for gambling. Now he fretted and worried; he had been so close! His imagination became inflamed; the triviality of the difference between the right number and the wrong one (After all, he had it! And then was fool enough to change it!) nagged and gnawed at his sense of himself. Why had he come so close? He thought somebody was working roots on him! Somebody was hoodooing him! He went to see a root doctor, who told him great changes were going to come. He couldn't keep the thought of all the money he might have won out of his mind. Everywhere he walked in the streets of the city he saw things that could have been his, had he not changed one small thing for another small thing! Automobiles, high yaller women, liquor in expensive cabarets, were all possibilities that hung within inches of his grasp! He tried gambling again, but had a streak of bad luck. The pressure of city life broke his spirit. Within two weeks he was back home, preparing to dedicate his life to the ministry, dedicated to fight against gambling, which had been the source of his great wisdom, and against hoodooing, which had failed to help him in a time of great need. His determination to fight against the small things that had insulted him was so great that he even took a job working in the woods, cutting crossties. One day, a saw cut off the little finger on his right hand. Because of his particular cast of mind, he hardly missed the finger, and my mother remembers his coming home after the accident in the best of humor.

As the years passed, he became a great and dignified preacher. His preoccupation was with the great issues, like God, White People, and His Family. This caused him to give everything a strange proportion. He would refer to the few books he had as his "library," and would often say to me or my brother, when he was puzzling over an important question, "Son, go into my library" and bring him a book he didn't have. Of course we would look at each other in bewilderment. Our mother took up for him and would say to us, "You know what he means."

"The reason looking at a woman's behind gives you pleasure," said Mr. Mott, a veteran of these discussions and expert on the loopholes of logic, "is because it puts you in the mind of what you already had once."

"No, that ain't the idea of the thing at all," Leon Bellow cut in. "What gives you pleasure about anything like that is the size of it; it got to be the right size, cause if it ain't, you don't even see it in the first place."

Now, the fact that my father had the ability to get all these men to answer something that everybody knew the answer to caused Dick Yoeman to stare at my father with the eye of one who thinks he is beholding before him the sight of an unearthly being.

"Please, Reverend," he said, "I swear, sometimes you make me feel like a woman!"

Bubble Bland, taking out a B.C. powder from his plaid shirtpocket, claimed that it was space and magnitude created by the distance of the faraway object itself, which stimulated the airy color of the imagination that gave pleasure to the sight of a woman's behind. "Man," he said, "when I was in jail, that was the only damn thing that I had to fall back on. Was thinking about a fine ass going 'long the road."

He dropped the B.C. in the corner of his lip, glanced at the reverend, and said, "That, and the Bible."

"Stop lying, Bubble," Leon said. "You ain't never been to jail. Who would put you in jail?"

"What do you know, jackass," he said, snapping at Leon. "Excuse me, Reverend, but look, you sissy, I was in jail before you was born. I been in more jails than you got fingers. I know you little punks think you mens now, huh?"

Mr. Mott shuffled seriously. Ignoring the bickering between the fat old man and young Leon, he picked up the main thread of Bubble's argument. "I think Bubble's got the idea behind the thing," he said. "Unless you see a woman's butt at a distance, it ain't nothing. Cause if you right up on the thing, you can't see it. Just like if a woman's got a big butt, like a lot of women, then it ain't pretty, cause you can't get your eyes around it. See, getting your eyes around it is the main idea, cause that's like putting your hands around it. When I was younger, and I'd be out with a gal, first thing I did when we got to the cemetery with the moon shining full overhead and everything still as warm air, is slide both of the hams right in my hand."

"I see the point you making," Blind Bronson said. "Being a blind man, I quite agree; everything really leads to the touch, the feel."

"Why," my father said, bringing the matter back into the realm of the serious, "does some butts, the high butt for example, give pleasure and the flat butt, for another example, does not? Why is it that when King Solomon looked at Sheba he was drawn to her posterior and not to the posterior of her maiden?" Lindsey began to imitate the women.

Everybody clapped their hands.

"Boy, you ought to be in one of them minstrel shows." Mr. Mott laughed. "Do the sway-back gal!"

He did the sway-back, the low-butt woman, the duck-back, and the no-butt woman.

"Let me see if you can do a white woman," Leon teased.

Lindsey threw his hat down on the ground and started walking like a white woman: long, corny flat-footed steps, her skirts swinging from side to side like a thin gossamer curtain in a strong wind, stomach sticking way out, shoulders careening from side to side, eyes cocked sideways at the niggers sitting on their steps . . . it was great.

Then, for an encore, he did Violet May and Juicy Belle, two of the finest sisters in our town. Juicy Belle was my favorite. She had the finest brown ass you ever wanted to see. I was in love with her. She wasn't but sixteen but she had all of her shit together. When I saw Lindsey imitating her walk, mincing his steps like a Chinese woman, imitating her little tiny waist that was so small you could get your hands round it and still have some left over, imitating her small little mouth that you could barely get your finger in, and those big coffee-cooling lips, and her painted fingernails, even the sound of her sandals slapping against the back of her heels as she strolled across the face of this godforsaken world, and even the jasmine smell of her body—when I saw my uncle imitating Juicy Belle's walk better than she could even do it herself, hot tears ran down my cheeks!

"That's good!" Leon was shouting. "Do Sarah Butler!" I saw my father smiling, and I believed, for the first time in a long time. Everybody was enjoying it.

"Do who?" Lindsey asked. Sweat was rolling down his face.

"Oh-oh, look younder who's coming. Trouble!"

Luke Martin drove by in his pickup truck.

Lindsey was in trouble because he was courting the same girl, Diana Shaw, that Luke Martin was courting. Diana Shaw wasn't white but was known to go out with white men. She was "ruint," Gramma Connie said. She was Old Man Jube's gal. Had Cherokee Indian blood in her, had white blood, had nigger, too. She was raised real nice, but she been an apple in the white folks' yard, Gramma Connie'd say. They said somebody saw her in Wilmington all dressed up with fine clothes and high-heel shoes with ribbons and painted up with talcum powder. She was fine. Lindsey couldn't stay away from her, though. And the white man Luke couldn't stay away from her neither.

Later that night at the juke joint, I heard Lindsey cuss him out. "Hey, white boy"—Lindsey laughed at him—"you can't come around here and get my woman. We can't go out to White Town and get your women, can we?"

Luke Martin stood at the bar, looking embarrassed as hell. Lindsey kept on laughing at him.

I'll never forget his laughter. Only a black man can laugh at a white man with that laughter.

Later that night, when I was at my grandmother's house, I heard: "Lindsey is dead! Luke Martin killed him!"

We all jumped into the car. The body was not more than a mile from my grandmother's house. He had been coming home. Lying in the grass on the side of Highway 211, his body was as motionless as if it had been discarded like the dry yellow newspaper that lay near him.

I felt my mother's arms around me, pressing tight. She burst out crying and let me go. Somebody—Mary Richardson I believe—grabbed me and my brother Buck and put her hands across our eyes. "Get the children! Don't let them see it," she muttered. But I had already looked, had seen his face, how half of it had been torn off. A blanket was thrown over the bottom part of his body, covering his groin. Somebody had carefully thrown it over that part—I never knew why. Evidently Luke Martin had hit him with his car and just driven on.

My point was the same, I thought. Lindsey was not Christ, as my uncle Gadge had portrayed him in his play; he was a stand-up comic, who laughed in a white man's face, and was killed for it, but through me, his nephew, he was still going to laugh.

As I looked in the mirror after drawing the curtain on the bit, I thought, ah, my true great artist, how you do respect the intelligence of your audience.

I got up and took a shower, got dressed and headed for the club.

# 9

THAT night on stage I was still too afraid to leave my routine, but I managed to get across some of my "message." I could not betray Lindsey. ". . . I once tried *not* to be a comic," I told them, "but I didn't have the willpower *not* to expose these impostors and hypocrites! They're everywhere. Things have gotten so bad that a friend of mine decided to sell his soul to the Devil. He called the operator to get the area code to Hell . . . The operator asked him, 'Where are you callin' from?" He said: 'Hollywood.' She said, 'That's a local number.' "

They knew what I was talking about and gave me a big hand. ". . . This town reminds me of my own home town back in the Deep South. Mr. Mose Tucker had him a nice business selling ice in the community. But this one sister kept buying her ice from the white man. One day somebody asked her why she kept buying her ice from the white man when Mr. Mose Tucker was selling it. The lady said, 'Well, I tell yo' the truf'—I tried 'em both and, you know, that white man's ice is just colder than that nigger's ice . . .' "

Somebody way in the back laughed with me. What I decided to do, then, was slip in one more about the South.

". . . Sort of reminds me of my Uncle Lindsey. My Uncle Lindsey was lazy . . . I ain't bullshitting you . . . He was the original lazy nigger that we've all been tryin' to get away from . . . right?"

A black bourgeois couple were sitting in the second row so I directed the joke to them.

78 |

". . . Lindsey was sleeping under a tree one day and this white man from the North came up to him. 'Say, my good fellow, what're you doin'?' Lindsey said, 'Restin'.' The white man said, 'Why don't you get busy and develop your fields?' Lindsey said, 'Why?' 'So you can make a lot of money.' Lindsey said, 'What good is money?' The white man said, 'Money will bring you leisure.' Lindsey said, 'What'll I do with leisure?' White man said, 'Then you can rest.' 'But why do all that,' Lindsey wanted to know, 'when I'm restin' now?' "

"My Uncle Lindsey was a very groovy guy—way ahead of his time. He was so hip that he had me believing that Jesus was a black woman with big tits and a big, well-stacked ass . . . that's right! Everytime he saw a fine black woman he'd look at her and go, 'JEEZ-US!' ' "

The house got really happy and gave me a big hand. "Thank you. G'night!"

I was still standing right there on the stage feeling like a cork bubbling up on one of them ocean waves. I knew I wasn't gonna get another laugh big as the one I done got, so decided to let it go. By now the people were clapping their hands big and loud enough to wake the dead. I saw a dude down in the front row put his fingers in his mouth and whistle a catcall. Right in the front row, all of them—the girl in the Midwestern scoop-up hairdo, the joker in the green polyester double knit, the two faggots from West Santa Monica with short crew-cut hairdos—can't quite get those long, broad smiles off their faces.

Placing the mike back in the stand, I said, "Thank you. G'night!" What'd I do that for? They started clapping louder than before now. Was I really funny? A couple guys were standing up in the back.

Now, as I'm coming off the stage through the path of tables and chairs and laughing people, they were gleaming up at me like I'm some kind of imperial chieftain. A hand reached out and grabbed mine, its owner saying, "Thank you, man!"

Long after he let my hand go I still felt the encouragement in his grip. By that gesture he'd laid an accolade on me, given me an award for my courageous feat, like I'd been out on the basketball court—Dr. Magic Johnson or somebody. I hit the end of the aisle where a lot of people were waiting from me. Dap was already on stage and over my shoulders I heard him —"Ladies and gentlemen, I've decided to give up part of my sex life. I'm trying to decide which half to give up: thinking about it or talking about it!"—but I'm still movin' very fast toward the broom closet.

I wasn't swift enough, though. A girl threw her arms around me as I hit the top steps to the dressing area and busted me on the lips with one of them big, juicy kisses that girls can give and nobody, not even faggots, can resist.

"You were *in-cread-dee-bull!*" she shouted and kissed me again. "I could NOT buleeeeve it!" turning to nobody in particular and going, "Do you believe this guy?" And then: "He's unbelievable! I mean, you were unbelievable! You really were!"

I looked at her—she looked like Jane Fonda and Catherine Deneuve rolled into one.

"What's your name?" I asked. I couldn't really think of anything else to ask. I was still pretty excited and everything. "Cheryl," she said.

That was funny, though, because practically every night I do my act I meet some chick and her name is always something like Cheryl. I just can't seem to get away from that type. Big titties. Shapely body. Blonde. Just ready to screw a comedian. Like me.

She leaned closer to me again. "Would you like a toot of coke?"

"Sure," I said, "but not here." We went over to her car— a nice little Porsche. When I really looked at her she was quite a fine lady.

Inside, she unfolded the white package of coke while I rolled a dollar bill into a tube.

"Did I ever tell you the one about the man with the small head?" I asked.

She threw her head back and laughed. "Oh, you don't know how much I love comedy. I got sexually aroused when I saw you on stage! I really did."

"A couple went into this restaurant and there was a good-looking guy sitting across from them. He was a very handsome dude but he had a very small head. So the girl said to her date, 'That's a very handsome dude, but what a small head,' and the guy she was with said, 'Oh, don't you know the story about him?' And she said, 'No, tell it to me.' Well, it seems that a long time ago this guy ended up on an island where he found this bottle in the sand. He opened the cork and a genie came out. The genie thanked him for saving her life and offered as his reward to grant any wish he might have. The genie was a real knockout, so the guy said, 'I'd like to sleep with you.' The genie said, 'I can't, I'm on my period,' and the guy said, 'Well, how about a little head!' "

Cheryl laughed so hard that I got a good glimpse at her full breasts without her noticing. I figured that if I kept telling jokes I'd end up in her pants.

She looked like a million girls you've seen before in *Playboy*. She was a modern goddess, an icon of our film age. Perfume exuded from her body and I wanted to kiss her red, full, smiling lips.

"I'd like to talk to you," I said, "but I'm not feeling well."

"Why? What's wrong," she asked, still smiling.

"I gotta lay down somewhere. Can we go to your house?" I was acting of course.

"Sure," she said, and turned the key in the Porsche. "Just tell me some more jokes."

I was acting, playing my favorite character, Mr. Jiveass Nigger, me. As the car swerved out into the street, a couple white boys walked around the car. They sneered at me, the very picture of an arrogant nigger with a pretty white woman, but sneer all you want, I thought.

"The lady who owns the club thinks I hate white people," I said to her. Thalia didn't think that, but I wanted to put Cheryl on. It was more fun when you put people on.

"You hate white people?" She laughed. "You're the kindest, the gentlest person I've ever met!"

"Well, that's what she told me," I said. "But I thank you for the kind words."

"They're crazy," she said, caressing the side of my face with her free hand. "I've never met anybody as friendly as you."

"Well, that's what she told me," I said. "I really appreciate that."

"Oh, it's no problem, believe me!" Cheryl said. "I'm just so happy to do anything for you. Know any more good jokes? I'm really getting turned on."

"A soul brother, from Midnight, Mississippi died," I said, ". . . and . . ."

"Oh, good!" Cheryl said. "Tell it . . ."

". . . died and went to heaven. When he got there he saw a door with 'White Only' on it and another one that said 'Colored.' When he went to St. Peter to complain, St. Peter said, 'Boy, whar yo' from?' Very proudly, the soul brother said, 'I'se from Mississippi, and I have you know, Brother St. Peter, that Mississippi's now *integrated*. Why, the colored goes to eat wid da whites in the restaurants. Dey goes to school wit' 'em. And as a matter of fact, just five minutes ago when I was alive, I was goin' into a white church to be *married* to a white woman!' Then the soul brother paused and started to scratching his head. 'What's the matter?' St.

Peter asked him. 'Well, as a matter of fack, dat wus the las' thing I remember!' "

She laughed. "You're very funny—not just on the stage."

"Jewish humor is very funny," I said, "because Jews went through a lot just like we black people did."

"That's true." Cheryl giggled.

"The only thing is, though," I said, "we went through it and then Jews went through it and we are still going through it! This Jewish guy once walked around the corner and ran into Hitler. Hitler said, 'See that pile of shit over there, Jew? Eat it!' So the Jew is eating the shit and Hitler starts laughing so hard that he drops the gun. The Jew grabs the gun and makes Hitler eat the shit. When he went home that night his wife said, 'So how was your day?' The Jew said, 'Darlin', you won't believe who I had lunch with today.' "

She lived in West Los Angeles, south of Westwood, west of the Santa Monica freeway, near the Nu-Art Theater, in a nonglamorous neighborhood that was so safe, she said, as we came into the apartment, "that I can empty the garbage in my bathrobe."

It was an apartment with hanging ferns and stained-glass windows, very chic.

"Make yourself comfortable," she said, "and I'll get us a cognac."

When she returned I asked her if I were right about her coming from the Midwest.

"No," she said, "I'm not from the Midwest. I'm from Pasadena. It is true that I'm an actress."

"Oh?"

"I'm on *General Hospital,*" she said, handing me my drink.

"What part do you play?"

"I'm a nurse," she said, "but I don't have more than a few lines."

She looked like the straightest Miss America. "Would you like to listen to some music?" she asked.

"What kind of music do you have?" I asked, expecting her to say the name of some country Western singer whose name I would vaguely know and whose music I would tolerate.

"Early Coltrane," she said.

I laughed.

She looked at me and smiled. "I told you that my straight look is very deceiving," she said. "I've loved jazz since college and I get turned on with black humor."

"What do you mean?" I asked her.

She leaned over and kissed me lightly and teasingly on the lips. "I mean that you made me hot when you were on stage," she said, getting up and going over to the record collection.

I watched her as she took out a Coltrane album and put it on the turntable.

"Is that why you wanted to get on stage?" I asked, watching her legs and thighs from behind.

She turned around when the sound of the soothing jazz exuded from the speakers. "I'm an exhibitionist," she said. "Haven't you picked that up yet?"

She sat down beside me on the sofa again. "I'm very horny tonight," she said.

"And so am I," I said.

"Was it true," she asked, "about how you got started in comedy?"

"Yes, you mean about Gramma Connie?"

"Yes?"

"Everything is true that I say on stage. The one thing that I didn't tell was about how Lindsey was killed. His death will always make me bitter. But not bitter about white people, but about life. That's why I like to perform. It takes away the bitter experiences."

Spreading her legs wider apart so that I could not miss the view of her panties, she smiled at me and licked her lips.

Trying to avoid the obvious, I went on to another joke. "A white man went to a black man. Said, 'When I fuck, my babies come out white, but when you fuck, they come out black. I want you to teach me how to make them come out black.' The black man said, 'I'll tell you how. When you make love with your wife, drink plenty of wine.' So the white man thanked him and went home and got drunk on wine, but when his wife had the baby it was still white. So he goes back to the black man and tells him. The black man said, 'Well, the next time you make love to her, put some grease on your dipstick.' So the white man came back and said he'd put grease on his dipstick but his children still came out white. 'Well, tell me this. What kind of dipstick you using?' In a whiney, femme, West Santa Monica, faggots' delivery: 'Jes my regular . . . old . . . dipstick.' 'Did you use a fourteen-inch dipstick?' 'No, why?' 'Was it four inches thick?' 'N . . . no.' 'Well, see that's your problem right there.' 'What?' 'YOU LETTING TOO MUCH LIGHT GET UP IN THERE!' "

Watching her throw her head back and laugh, I felt power over her body as I laid my hand on her hot thigh. I kissed her, and suddenly forgot all of the anger I'd felt a few minutes before.

I sucked her delicious tongue in my mouth and cupped her swelling breasts in my hand, gently rubbing the hardening nippers between my fingers. I heard her moan as I pulled her closer into my embrace. Pushing my hand up her dress, I felt her smooth sun-baked thigh. With the tip of my fingers I caressed the moisture through her pubic hair until I had my fingers as deep as they would go inside her pussy. She was so hot she got up and led me to the bedroom without a word. She clicked on a light, displaying a bed with a mirror. She pulled her dress over her head, revealing a long thin body in panties and bra, which she quickly slipped out of as I watched. She laid down on the bed with her legs open and her eyes closed. I thought of all the white motherfuckers I could get revenge on as I bent my head down on her wet throbbing pulsating vagina. I took the clitoris between my lips and flicked it with my tongue at the beat of a congo drum, running her mad with pleasure. When I penetrated her I stood back and held my dick, thinking, *If those white motherfuckers could see me now they'd blow their own brains out!* I eased down between her long, creamy thighs and sank in. She gave a moan and started screaming loud every time I pushed in and out.

"Tell me a joke," Cheryl said suddenly.

"What? Are you kidding? Right now?"

"Yes! Just when I'm about to come! Tell me a joke! Be funny!"

I was pumping away at her firm white ass. "I can't be funny now! I'm *fucking* you!"

She grabbed my shoulder so tight that I felt her nails tearing into my skin. "I'm gonna come! Tell me a joke," she screamed. I could feel her orgasm coming on like a thousand bulls.

"Be FUNNY!" she bellowed. "I'M GONNA COME!"

"I can't think of a joke right now," I whispered. I couldn't. I couldn't think of anything.

"Tell me a joke. I want to laugh and come TOGETHER!" she was begging me.

"Once . . ." I banged my nuts against her raised, tight white ass. "Once . . . there was a . . ."

"Oh, please go on . . ." she moaned. ". . . Oh, you making me COME!"

". . . A Jew! . . ."

". . . Squirt your come in the bottom of my pussy, baby!"

". . . And a black man . . .!"

". . . Fuck my pussy, Drum . . ."

". . . And a white man . . ."

". . . Come in my cunt . . .!"

". . . They all went to heaven . . .!"

". . . *I* am in HEAVEN TOO! I'M COMING! Oh, MY God, I'm coming!"

". . . Can you wait for the punch line?"

". . . I CAN'T WAIT! HA, HA, HA! You are FUNNNNYYYY AND I'M COMING!"

She came for about three minutes. When she was finished, I asked her why she wanted me to tell jokes while she had an orgasm.

"I always wanted to have a comic orgasm, you know," she said, "come while I was being balled by a comedian."

"And you picked me?"

"WELL, you're funny, aren't you?"

# 10

I didn't feel funny.

I got Cheryl up to drive back to my car parked in front of the Comedy Club. And I said good night to her. I never saw her again.

But there was always a girl from Nebraska who was starting an acting career who had some coke and drove a brand-new Porsche, and always I'd go home with her if I chose, and always would fuck all the rest of the night. This was the life I loved as a comedian.

This was the middle of the trash bin in America.

This was Walt Whitman's "America!"

This was where the dreams and nightmares are indistinguishable!

This was Kafka's *Amerika!*

Oh! Elegant bullshit! Is not Hollywood not your home town! This was the place where thousands of us are driven each year to find a dream that we finally find out never existed at all! We believed in its existence only out of the pain we suffered elsewhere! The pain of the rest of America made us believe that Hollywood existed! It had to exist! If you see your uncle unjustly killed by whites in the South you make Hollywood an El Dorado, a fantasy land where glamour and personal celebrity lift you from the cruel implacable jaws of injustice to the heights of etherized exclusivity. If there was no justice in America, at least pleasure would drive out its pain.

As I inserted my key in the door, a disgusting feeling came

over me. I didn't know if it was an abominably dark thought of Lindsey's ignoble death or the stupefied sex with Cheryl or my proud outburst against Thalia or a combination of all three, but I was suddenly aware of being thrown into a deep pit of depression.

Aunt Lottie was waiting for me. An overprotecting mother, she was too good to me and that made staying with them ever more painful. I closed the door behind me without causing the slightest sound: clowns can be as quiet as a cat walking on fur sometimes.

Using a night-light that illuminated the dark hallway leading to the bedrooms as a guide, I cautiously avoided a noisy collision with the furniture. Reaching the hallway, I tiptoed down it toward my bedroom, but as I passed my uncle and aunt's bedroom I saw that the door was ajar and the bedside lamp was on.

In this brief glance, I read yet another unhappy chapter in the miserable life of this respectable couple. My aunt was reading a book; the place beside her—where Uncle Gadge was supposed to be—was deserted. That empty space meant that Uncle Gadge was out indulging his gambling habits. An image of him sitting at a table with a gram of cocaine at one elbow came to mind, and the cackling laughter of some prostitute at the other elbow.

Just as I was about to turn away she suddenly looked up —she must've heard me come into the hall—and gave me the most pitiful stare I'd ever seen. It really got to me. By the time I got to my room, all I could do was go for the bed. I lay down a few minutes, just thinking what an unlucky asshole I was. "Oh, I'm so miserably depressed!" I wanted to cry out.

I might have felt different about my situation had the women in Hollywood been different, but they were a special breed that doesn't exist anywhere else in the world. Unfeeling and cold-blooded as a dead fish on ice, the woman of Hollywood was beautiful as a silent-screen movie star; and

I was attracted to this hollow image because it elevated my emotions coolly out of my own confused identity, giving me a Clark Gable self-image. The woman of Hollywood sees herself—not in the mirror, but on the movie screen. Her color and style of dress, her every minute gesture, the way she flutters her eyelids, the tilt of her head that can run a man crazy with passion, the way she walks in the long skirts with the slits up the side, the way she blows out cigarette smoke —so nonchalantly—the clichés she mouthes over oyster shells in fashionable restaurants, the witty interjections after lovemaking, her entire philosophy of politics, poetry, love, economics, blasé manner of painting her face in public places, her soulless lovemaking, the way she worships herself, a base slave to luxury and stupidity and arrogance in various plots—all this she imitates from her celluloid mirror, the movie screen. The movie screen's effect is to decrease one's own reality for the dream world of fantasy, and the woman of Hollywood outstrips everybody else in making this her reality. Consequently, the woman of Hollywood has no reality of her own. She may have come from Harlem or Watts or the coal mines of Pennsylvania, she may have escaped the slums of Chicago or Houston, but when she arrives in Hollywood she dons the external images of the cinematic mirror and social consciousness. It doesn't matter if she's young or old, black or white, Chinese or Irish, tall or short, fat or slim, Jew or gentile, Islamic or Christian—she is beautiful and that's all that matters in her self-image. Sometimes she's an old, wrinkled beldame with a dozen face-lifts, bejeweled and coiffeured in the latest, making one last and desperate grasp at a lost youth; sometimes she's a young girl, barely out of her teens, already an expert at the despicable wiles of whoring, burning with wet desire and lustful ambition to be ranked as the equal of her superiors in vice; but always she's the woman—excuse me—lady of Hollywood.

There are two ways to sleep with the woman of Hollywood,

I thought. The first is to be rich. But if you're broke, as I usually was, you'd have to be able to make them laugh. You'd have to be in show business. If you told a really funny joke, then the woman of Hollywood would congratulate herself on having discovered your talent, which would become a promissory note, and so she'd laugh. I just lay there, sinking happily into my misery, my *delectatio morosa.*

I could feel myself slipping into a deep, dark, bottomless well of depression. I needed a cigarette. The thought suddenly sprang into my mind like a solution. I found my package. There was one cigarette left. I looked at it a long time before I lit it up, however.

I hated myself also for not being able to move out for another week and give Uncle Gadge and Aunt Lottie their space. I felt like an intruder, especially since I knew how unhappy Lottie was.

I looked around the room again with loathsomeness in my very soul. Would I ever get away from this disgustingly sick self-image?

I decided that I'd go down to the liquor cabinet and steal a bottle of Scotch and get some ice cubes and soda and bring it all back up to my room and get plastered. That made good sense to me. Since I was going to get depressed anyway, why not get depressed and drunk? Depressingly drunk—or drunk depressingly. The idea appealed to me so much that I thought for a moment, that maybe I wouldn't get depressed after all. Perhaps all I needed was a good stiff drink.

But before I go downstairs, I told myself, what I need is another cigarette. I thought I had an extra pack somewhere in the room. I went through the things on the top of the bureau and then pulled out one of the drawers. The only thing in it was a batch of newspaper clips and an old package of Trojans. Beneath the Trojans was an article on me from the summer I spent in San Francisco. I started to push the drawer closed but something made me stare at that article.

I was drawn to it, and yet I knew if I read it, it would make me even more depressed. The story was about a part of my past which I did not want to deal with at all, but which I knew, had I the courage to reread it, would put me on to the road to rebirth, to recovery.

I put on my blue bathrobe and went to the kitchen. The morning light was rubbing its azure back against the windowpanes, and the kitchen was clean as a monastery. Opening the liquor cabinet, I saw a bottle of Scotch and two bottles of bourbon, one half full and one sealed. I took the unopened one. My uncle was rich, I decided self-righteously, he could afford it. Anyway, it was cheaper for him to buy me a bottle of bourbon to kill my depression with than get me a job acting in the studio where he was so well loved by the whites. Pulling open the automatic ice dispenser, I grabbed a couple handfuls of those little ice cubes and threw them into a big bowl I found on the yellow tiled counter, plucked a glass down from the shelf, and started out of the kitchen; but just as I was cruising past the bar I spied a wooden bowl containing packages of potato chips and beer nuts. I swiped those too.

As I was making my way down the hallway again, I heard my aunt moan and call out, "Gadge, is that you?" and I paused before I answered, "No, it's me—Jonah." I wanted to say, "It's me about to get over my depression with alcohol, why don'tcha join me?" but thought better of it, and added: "He'll be home soon, I think?" She didn't even answer me, or anything.

I went on into my room, and put my booty down on the chair in front of my bed. I poured myself a big, stiff drink, and took the first swallow, feeling the liquor anesthetize my lonely pain. It seemed as if everything I'd try to do in my short life had ended in failure. I remembered all the women I'd loved who had eventually scorned me. If I died today the only people who would cry would be my family and the only reason they would cry would be because they were obliged to cry. In my twenty-two years on earth I had made no impression on anybody. I'd traveled the world but I'd not gotten anywhere with the world, or myself. I'd just left the South, just seen my father, and had realized that I could never live there again. Now I was in Los Angeles, the capital of show business, and yet I couldn't do the kind of comedy I wanted to.

Out of the corner of my eye, I caught a glimpse of that newspaper article. I reached over and picked it up. Just looking at it made me laugh—laugh so that I wouldn't cry. I started reading it. When I'm drunk I can read anything—even stuff about myself. The liquor gives me assurance about myself that I do not have without it. Entitled, "COPS DON'T FIND COMIC FUNNY," the article was published in the *Phoenix*, Wednesday, July 8, 1980; the day after I was arrested for obscenity on the U.C. Berkeley campus. At the top of the article is a photo of me in the middle of my stand-up act, with five hundred students laughing in the background. I'm wearing my dashiki—gold and purple—and my natural is big and well kept, and I'm in blue denims and sandals. Also in the picture are two campus cops approaching me from both sides. On the faces of the students—if you look closely—you can see pity, real genuine pity for me. It's not any jive pity—but real human pity—the kind of pity Aristotle talked about. After all, they are not about to get their asses thrown in jail. They knew more than I did what was about to happen to me. So that's my definition of pity: being sorry about something horribly painful happening to somebody else that couldn't possibly happen to you. The caption beneath this picture reads: "Jonah Drinkwater shouting obscenities before being thrown off campus."

I put the newspaper down and took another long drink from the glass of bourbon, my nepenthe, wondering at the mystery of my pain. How had this happened to me, *how?* It seemed only yesterday that I was a child entertaining my father with my mail-order catalogue magic, my boyish ingenuity. What had happened between those innocent boyish desires to entertain my father and the time the police locked me up in the county jail for telling the truth? I still was the same person, the same Jonah.

My glass was empty and I refilled it desperately; the first paragraph of this "eternal bulletin" told the whole story: "Campus police arrested an impromptu comic yesterday shortly after he began a performance in front of the Student Union during his second appearance here in three days."

It was a beautiful summer day, as I remember the incident. Overhead, the blue sky stretched out to eternity. A single cloud floated by. There were no clouds of ambition in this sky; this was not a Hollywood sky yet . . . clouds of chance that grown people chase.

The Berkeley campus was full of students, everywhere pretty girls smiled at you as you passed. I had just arrived in San Francisco to begin my career as a comedian with the campus as my stage. I stopped in front of the Student Union, where a group of street artists were selling their wares of pottery, handmade jewelry, batik and tie-dye shirts, ceramic earrings, leather sandals, and coats with fringe on the sleeves; on the corner a fortune-teller had set up her business. On another corner an impromptu jazz group consisting of a white boy blowing an old saxophone held together with rubber band and glue, a black boy playing a washtub drum, and a white girl playing a child's ukulele amplified by a homemade speaker. As I began my act I noticed my competition approaching: a Hare Krishna group came toward me chanting and beating tambourines. As if they weren't enough, behind them came a religious fanatic, chanting slogans from the Bible. Wearing a checkered too-tight suit, this freckled zealot wandered among the students chanting maxims from the Bible. Behind the zealot came a campus transsexual who had been one of the university's leading psychologists until he flipped out one day and came on campus wearing a dress and long unbecoming earrings and delivering a seriocomic speech about the advantage of hating people overtly as a provable cure for neurosis. Behind him came a group of ROTC cadets. Just as they were about to pass me, I shouted an insult out at them. This is the way I begin my act—usually with an insult. "Hey! Look at those ROTC jerks! There are the fuckers that went to Vietnam! They're ready to go any fucking where and kill people. Look at them!" I broke off and started imitating their stupid walk. A pretty girl started laughing. I had my first audience of the day. I got back up the steps and continued: "We have to realize who the enemy is. Those fuckers will one day be killing people in the Third World so that you and I can live in luxury! They're going to be the army officers who send black marines to Africa, India, Iran, Thailand to exploit other dark people so you can still call yourselves white!"

The young girl laughed again and looked around for approval from the other girl with her; they both giggled.

Just then, the checkered-suit-wearing zealot appeared in my range of sarcasm. "And look at him," I quipped. "This guy's telling us to 'Come unto the Lord,' and I wonder how long it's been since he *came!*"

The girls giggled again and nudged each other—students are really a horny bunch of individuals, quiet as it's kept, and any mention of sex gets their attention.

". . . This guy hasn't had any pussy since pussy had him . . . Look at him! See? . . . That's what happens to you when you don't fuck! So my message to you students is: Fuck! . . . Fuck as much as you can! Fuck and laugh as much as you can!"

As soon as I said "Fuck" the crowd began to swell with curious, grinning faces. A tall, blond-headed boy turned away and shouted, "Screw you!" and started walking away, giving me a great opportunity to bring in my next subject: fraternities. ". . . Look at Mr. Straight . . . he must be a fraternity boy, huh? You know who they're going to be when they grow up, right? They will be our businessmen of tomorrow. And are they dumb . . . All they do is sit around and drink beer and talk about a girl's tits and ass. 'Hey, did you see the knockers on Sue-Ann?' These are jerks who will be telling you what to do in five years. They will tell the ROTC guys to go kill somebody in another country so they can sell their businesses . . . and drink some more beer and tell about some girl's ass!"

The crowd was laughing and applauding me now. Just then a group of students came by carrying a banner that read: "U.S. OUT OF EL SALVADOR!" I yelled, "Right on!" and they waved back, "Right on, brother!" The audience ate that up and started applauding too. I went into my prop bag and brought out my pink pig and threw it down on the ground. The pink pig was the biggest piggybank I could find and I'd put a pair of movie-star glasses on him, giving him the aura of a celebrity. Then I took out an American flag and waved it as I addressed the pig. ". . . Hello, Ronnie, my name is Joe America. Oh, Ronnie, we really love you, we want to help you cut off food stamps and job programs so Nancy can redecorate the bathrooms in the White House."

The students went mad with laughter at my satire.

Suddenly the blond-headed fellow came rushing through the crowd and snatched up my pig. I grabbed him by the shoulder and turned him around and snatched the pig back. "Listen, motherfucker, you can't do that! This is my act!" I shouted at him. "This is my fucking pig!"

He turned to me with the reddest face I'd ever seen in my life. "If you don't like it here in America, why don't you go back to Africa!" he screamed at me.

"Why don't you go the fuck back to Germany and stop fucking with my act!"

He pushed me back and I almost fell and that really pissed me off. I jumped up and reached for him and he socked me against the jaw. But I caught him by the leg and kicked him.

"Get him! Get him!" I heard somebody shouting and I didn't know if they meant me or him.

Somebody else said, "Get the police! Get the police!" and then I heard somebody say, "The police are coming!" and I grabbed my pig and was putting him in the prop bag when I looked up and saw the police coming in my direction. The crowd had grown larger now that some live action was being enacted in front of them. But I wasn't going to be waiting around to see what would happen when the police got there. I headed off toward the library, hearing the crowd shouting over my shoulder, "He hit him! I saw it!"

When I got to the library, I turned and saw the cop following me at a running gait. I started running faster then. Coming to the corner of the library, I cut it so fast that it must've seemed like I went into the stone wall.

Two days later I was back on campus doing my act when I got arrested. The same blond-headed student appeared with a policeman and accused me of beating him the previous day.

The second paragraph of the article said: "Jonah Drinkwater, 22, of Berkeley, was booked and is being held in Alameda County Jail, charged with unlawfully returning to the campus after being told not to come back here within 72 hours. Drinkwater, who is scheduled to be arraigned this morning, faces a maximum fine of $500 or six months in jail."

What I didn't know at the time of my arrest was that I was being arrested under a law enacted in 1968 during two campus student strikes to ban speakers for three days if they were thought to be likely to interfere with campus activities. In the first place, I was not a "speaker" but a "satirist." "The comic," the article went on to say, "used obscene language and directed it toward the police, a police spokesman said."

That was true. Every time the cop put his hands on me to arrest me, I cussed him out. The students went wild with applause for me. They jibed at the cops and threw paper cups at them, but that just made the cops more determined to arrest me.

"Get your stuff," the cop said. The audience of about five hundred kids looked on. They were on my side; they were booing the cops for taking me away.

I reached down to pick up my pig prop. "I'm getting my pig," I shouted out at the audience. "Pig!"

"Right on!" the crowd screamed back.

Somebody else said, "That's bee-yuuuuuu-tiful!"

"I leave with this message from Apostle Paul!" I shouted to them as the cop led me handcuffed through the crowd. "I speak to you as a fool because the fool is the only person who enjoys the privilege to tell the truth without causing offense!"

A wild shout of support went up from the students as they followed the policemen, who had me in their grip as if I were a common criminal, across the campus.

We passed the check-suited zealot, who was raving at the students like a madman: "Christ is coming—repent!"

"Look at him—he's doing the same thing I'm doing and you're not arresting him!" I screamed at my persecutors, but the cops' only response was to squeeze a pair of handcuffs on my wrist.

But I couldn't stop shouting the truth at them. "He's the one who told me what Apostle Paul said."

One of the cops said, "Yeah, what did Apostle Paul say?" I thought he was serious, so I explained.

"He said, 'I come as a fool because only a fool can speak the truth and not cause offense.' And, officer," I pleaded, hoping he would listen to me, "that's all I was doing—just what you see that old religious fanatic doing."

The cop said: "Well, the difference is that he really is a fool and he ain't offending anybody, but you ain't a fool. You know exactly what you're doing and you're offending a lot of people—including me, 'cause I'm a Catholic. Now get in the fucking car!"

As they were stuffing me into the backseat of the campus police car, I saw a flower vendor looking at me with this incredible scowl on his face. That really hurt me—that scowl —because I'd always pictured flower vendors as my friends, but this guy looked at me and went "YEEUCK!" and then he spat on the ground.

They slammed the door shut but the window was still down.

"What do you mean by 'YEEUCK'?" I asked the flower vendor. "I didn't mean to offend *you*, man."

"I enjoy satire," he said, "but you make me puke! Even Richard Pryor and Mort Sahl know when to stop, you creep!"

As the car was pulling off, I saw the face of a pretty girl.

"It was you! It was you!" she yelled at me, but there was no anger in her voice, there was something else: appreciation, maybe, or wonderment. Her face was so pure and happy that I carried it with me to jail.

They booked me under the 1968 law as they had many student activists—inciting to riot. I was stripped of my street clothes, mugged, given a rubber mat to sleep on, and when I opened my mouth to ask a question, the officer who said he was a Catholic slapped me across the face. Then he looked guilty and I saw the guilt in him and he got mad again, and started hitting me across the head, and when I bent over he kicked me on the back, and I fell to the floor. I decided then and there that Apostle Paul might have been right about fools not causing offense two thousand years ago, but he was sure to get his ass kicked if he came back today.

In the middle of the night they brought a big black man into the cell across from me. He cussed out all the guards for about two hours. Finally he called one of them over to his cell. The officer came over and the big black man threw something in his face. The yellow stuff splattered all over the guard's face. It was only when the guard started wiping it off that I realized that it was shit. The big man roared with laughter, and soon every one of the prisoners was laughing. Even as they took that big black prisoner out to beat him, we were laughing. It was the most exhilarating laughter I've ever heard—pure rebellious laughter of the oppressed.

They let me out the next morning, and when I stepped out into the daylight—you don't know what a wonderful thing daylight is until you've spent the night in the county jail.

I read the article. Most of the time the reporter quoted the flower vendor, who said I was "obscene . . . disgusting . . . sickening . . . abhorrent . . ."

I knew something was wrong with our country then. I saw how easy it was to be treated abusively by the police for speaking the truth, and to go to jail and not be heard of again. I saw how easy it was for students to laugh at the truth of my comedy and then go on to their classes, and never think about me again, except when they needed another laugh. I knew how easy it was for a newspaper to distort my art, my humor, my insight. I saw how easy it was for the white police to take everything I said about religion and television and fraternities and student apathy and turn it against me.

I had gone to Ninevah to preach, and been swallowed by that Leviathan called the experience of the real world, but Uncle Gadge got me out of that whale by purchasing me a ticket to Los Angeles. Now I was swallowed up by this experience, but once out of it, I was going to be a better man. Already I could taste the sand from where this whale would beach me. Already I was anxious to yield to whatever experience living at the Fountain Lanai had waiting for me.

I sat there on the bed and poured the last of my uncle's bourbon into the glass. Just as I looked up I saw a package of cigarettes—the ones I'd been looking for—under my hat on the dresser. I leaped up and opened them and fired up one right away.

As I was lying there I heard Uncle Gadge coming home. I heard him coming into the living room, then down the hallway, and into the bedroom. I heard him undressing and getting into bed, and I heard my aunt's angry voice, asking him where he'd been.

# The Demi-Monde

# Monde

—

# 11

ABOUT a week after I'd moved into the Fountain Lanai, I was leaning over our balcony after work one afternoon when one of my neighbors, Celeste, drove her green MG into the entrance and stopped at the mailbox. I watched the door to see how far I could see up her skirt when she got out. A dark chocolate cupcake complexion, her body was slim and shapely. She was the only person I had talked to since I moved in. She was about twenty-five and told me she worked in the Salon de Beauté on Santa Monica.

A warm, heavy hand on my shoulder made me spin around. Tull grinned behind me. "You like her, eh?"

"Yeah. Why are you laughing? She has an old man?"

Leaning his head stupidly, he scratched it clownishly, and shot an ironical laughter into the golden-tinged smog. "How can I put it? She's not a sister . . . she's a . . . brother."

As she returned my lustful gaze, I now realized something was artificial about her beauty all the time. Too late, though. My mind kept saying no, while my eyes kept saying yes. That such charm could be fraudulent was hard to swallow.

"You don't believe it? What yuh doin'? Come with me to Gussie's," Tull said when he saw me staring. He grabbed my arm and we went down to Gussie's apartment. A white plate announced: Manager.

The manager's apartment distinguished itself from the other apartments in nothing except the peculiar taste of its inhabitant, a light-skinned brother in his early forties. Gussie had quite a handsome face, but he wasn't the type of person you'd want to know it.

"Go get the *Penthouse*," Tull instructed him with a laugh.

"What? He didn't know Celeste was a dude?" He looked at me, laughed, and disappeared into the bedroom. He emerged with the batch of *Penthouse* magazines. When he came to the one he was looking for, he flipped through it, offering me and Tull his shoulder to look over. "See? Look at that?" he said, thrusting the magazine into my face.

Yes, there she was. Old Celeste. A tall sister in a yellow bikini. While I looked at the picture, Tull and Gussie took turns throwing themselves on the floor and rolling on their backs laughing at me. After they had had a good laugh, Gussie offered us some wine.

"Celeste has already been on *The Dating Game*," Gussie explained in a blasé voice. "And *won*. See that white boy," he said. Now he was pointing out the window to an ordinary-looking white boy passing just at that moment. "That's her old man. Brothers, she can't pull the wool over," he said, forgetting completely the wool she'd just pulled over me. "Now look at this one?"

His stare out the window once again drew our attention to an inhabitant. This one, another tall blonde, wore a gray flannel suit, high heels, and carried a briefcase.

Tull teased Gussie about her. "Ask him her name," he said to me, laughing. "He won't tell you. He's been jamming her."

"I don't make it with my tenants," Gussie said.

Tull bent over and laughed.

"I'm not a dog," Gussie maintained. "Like you."

We sat there for a while. Occasionally Tull would remember the joke and laugh. We sat there looking out the window until a white boy came up on the balcony and walked by the window.

"Hey! Mike!" Gussie called out to him. "Come here!" The white boy stopped and came back to the door and opened it.

"What's the matter with you? You ain't speaking!"

Mike said, "I just got a lot of stuff to do. Hey, what's happenin'?"

"Come in, man, and close the door," Gussie said. "I want you to meet somebody."

Mike came in and closed the door.

"This is Jonah," Gussie said, "A new tenant. Jonah tried to hit on Celeste. He thought she was a fine sister!"

"He did? He didn't know?" Then Mike gave me a stupid look and then laughed, too. Old Gussie got the biggest kick off that joke.

"Anybody know where I can get some Quaaludes?" Mike asked.

"You try Sultan?" Gussie asked.

"No," Mike said.

"Knock on his door," Gussie said. "He just got a new shipment in."

Mike rose. "Yeah, I'll do that." He nodded at me. "Nice meeting you. I guess I'll be seeing you around then," he said and left.

"That white boy can play the blues, man," Gussie said as he rolled up a joint, "just, just like a black man."

"Remember a novel *King Kong's Revenge?*" Gussie said, looking at the brother who knocked on the window, grinned at us, and then came in the door. "This guy wrote it," Gussie explained. "He's a writer, Berkeley. Use to be one of those crazy-ass radicals."

"Hey, what's happenin'?" the tall brown-skinned brother said, standing in the door.

"Randell," Gussie said, "I want you to meet somebody, a new tenant—Jonah."

I got up and shook the brother's hand. His glasses made him look like an egghead.

"Jonah's a comedian," Gussie said, handing Randell the joint he'd just rolled up.

"Yeah," Randell said, taking the joint.

"You want some wine?" Gussie offered him.

"Yeah," Randell said and sat down on the sofa.

"Hey, man, Randell is a writer," Gussie volunteered. "He had his picture in the L.A. *Times!*"

"Naw, Gussie," Randell said abasedly. "Please."

"The man may not want the world to know everything about him," Tull joked in his defense.

Gussie said, "If he didn't want anybody to know about it, he shouldn't've let them put his picture in the *Times.* I saw it myself."

Randell looked at me and smiled.

The door opened and a big black Goliath stood in it.

"Man, come in and close the door," Gussie shouted. "Moose, did you bring some wine?"

Moose pulled a bottle of wine out of the paper sack and set it down on the table.

"What you think this is?" Moose said.

"This is Jonah. My new roommate," Tull said. "This is Moose. The people's poet."

Like the reggae fans, Moose sported a red Rastafarian. He wore a red-striped polo shirt, suspenders, and cowboy boots.

"Nice meetin' you, Jonah."

"Nice meetin' you, too."

He gave Gussie a record.

"Can you play the side with Joe Williams singing 'Lush Life'?" Moose said to Gussie.

"This chump didn't know that Celeste was a *male* female," Gussie said to Moose and Randell as he took the record and prepared to put it on the stereo.

"What? He didn't?" Moose laughed from where he had sat down as soon as he had handed Gussie the record. He looked comfortable and relaxed.

Randell chuckled and gave me a sizing-up look. He smiled quickly, and he reminded me somehow of my uncle Lindsey.

"Well," he said, winking at me, "give him a break," he said. "After all, he doesn't have the larceny in him as you two have!"

It was the first time I'd ever heard that word used. Gussie and Moose laughed.

I looked over at Tull. He glanced up at me just then and laughed, too.

For a few moments the four of us sat in a brotherly silence that Joe Williams filled up with the most beautiful love. Finally, apropos of nothing, Randell said, "That Joe Williams can sing 'Lush Life,' can't he?"

"It's the Mack's national anthem!" Gussie blabbed.

"But," continued Randell, "he can't sing it like Johnny Hartman can!"

"Johnny Hartman can't sing like this, man. Are you crazy? This is Joe *Williams.*"

"My man Johnny Hartman will make this sound like some high-school cheerleaders, man! Be serious!"

Gussie was very amused by the play animosity between Moose and Randell. They were more his friends than they were his tenants. I didn't know how to take Randell and Moose's shouting at each other at first.

"They're always arguing like this," Tull explained.

"Celeste is between a male and female," Randell said, looking up at me as he passed the joint. "Like everything in this town—everything is between its two extremes."

"What do you mean?" I asked him, taking a drag of the Colombian. This was going to be the perfect place to live.

"We, for example, are living between the two extremes," he went on. "On one side is Beverly Hills and on the other side of us is the ghetto. We're in the middle."

"I want to get back into the ghetto!" Moose complained.

"Well, go! It's still your choice," Randell told him with a stern look.

"I would but I've committed myself to this plan. One thing

I learned in the joint was not to go back on your word. I gave the organization my word. The matter is closed."

"Fine," Randell said. "Then we'll see what happens tonight."

Gussie fed my inquisitive look with a thoughtful laugh. "You don't know what we're talking about, do you?"

I laughed and said I didn't.

"Tonight there's a meeting of the Media Forum."

Randell looked. "Why don't you come with us?"

"What is it about?" I asked.

"It's the largest organized black coalition in the entertainment business," Randell said. "Tonight we are going to hear views and opposing views on whether to picket a film at Democracy Studios."

"Yes, I want to come," I said. "You wanna go, Tull?"

"Yeah, sounds like a plan," Tull said.

"What time is it?" Gussie said, looking out the window, "Look at this fool!" Another white guy was carrying a garbage can. "That's Derek," he explained, "an actor from New York. Every day about five, he empties Howard's garbage. You know why? Because Howard is the casting director at Universal. Ha-hahaha—and then on Saturdays he washes his car. He hopes one day Howard will get him a job! These actors are a trip, man!"

A Mercedes 450 pulled up by the mailbox and a blonde got out and left the car running.

"There's Esmeralda," Tull said, and Gussie turned to the window. She got back into the car and drove into the garage. Then she reemerged from the garage and came up the steps. She was wearing a green skirt with a long slit up the side and a yellow blouse. She went into an apartment on the first floor.

"She's an exhibitionist," Gussie announced. "She just likes to make love with her vibrator with the window open. There's nothing wrong with that. This apartment house is liberated. I let people do anything they want to do. And another thing, Jonah, I don't want anybody going over to those apartments unless the girls invite you over. Okay?"

Tull laughed. "He's okay, just a bit soft in the brain."

We watched Esmeralda walk through the rooms into the bedroom and take off her blouse.

"There it goes! The vibrator comes out!" Tull said, standing in the window following the movements of Esmeralda as she reached into a drawer and pulled out the longest white vibrator I'd ever seen. She was down to her panties and bra.

"Now the music," Tull said as we saw her turn on the radio near her bed.

"Now the pillow." She fluffed a pillow and then laid back on the bed, with her head disappearing in the pillow.

Gussie drew the curtains.

"If you want to watch her," he said, "go do it from your own room. I should be charging you admissions. Yeah, a dollar a head." He chuckled.

Just then a short woman in her fifties appeared by the mailbox.

"There's that damn Janet," Gussie muttered and went out on the balcony. "Janet," he called, "I'm kicking you out! Janet, did you hear me! I want you out of this building by Saturday!"

Janet ignored him and stepped out onto the street. Gussie came back in.

"She's bringing the reputation of this building down," he said. "The Hudsons are respectable people and if they see that bitch down on the streets carrying on like she does, they're going to leave. And if they leave, I'm going to have to pack it in."

Tull said, "Why don'tcha just leave her alone, Gussie?"

"Nigger, I'm the manager here," Gussie reminded him. "You don't tell me how to run my building. My Irish-American boss told me he likes the way I run the building. I am cruel. I kick out anybody I think should go. And the scum like Janet has got to go. Every week she pulls the same shit, getting drunk and dancing naked on the street. She reflects badly on the rest of us. And the Hudsons are respectable people. They paying two thousand dollars for that condominium! If they get wind of that bitch's carrying-on, they'll split."

Right-angling my shoulders, I shot a shaft of light into Gussie's irrational obsession. "What's the big idea, Gussie? What do the Hudsons think of the rest of this scum and scab? What do they think of your next-door neighbor, one of the biggest dealers in West Hollywood? What do they think of Esmeralda?"

We laughed at Gussie, but he could only grin at it distantly and mutter, "Fuck you niggers. I might kick all of you out."

That made us laugh louder then. I felt good about being able to joke with them. I was one of them now. A knock came to the door and Gussie said come in. Celeste appeared in the door all dressed up.

"Hi, fellows," she said brightly.

"Come in, Celeste," Gussie said, waving his hand in my direction. "Meet our new tenant."

When she shook my hand, I felt her flesh was dry and heavy like a man's hand.

"We've already met," she smiled to Gussie, "and this is my rent check." Gussie took the check and went to his office, which was a desk he had arranged just off from the kitchen.

"So are you tryin' to get into the business?" Celeste asked me politely.

She was dressed in a green blouse with a couple buttons undone. She had big tits just like a woman and she crossed her legs so that her short black skirt didn't ride up her long shapely legs just like a woman.

While I talked to her, Tull, Moose, Randell, and Gussie

were snickering behind their hands clasped over their mouths.

"No," I told her, "I'm a comic."

"Oh, that's just great," she said as she laid down an album she brought with her.

Tull picked up the album and looked at it. "Oh, I see Ritual has another album out," he said.

"Child, this one cut you got to hear is so hot! This girl is really smoking on this album," Celeste said re-crossing her legs.

Tull handed me the album. It had a picture of the famous disco singer, Ritual Bondage. With her hair short cropped, her broad squared shoulders, her stern evil-looking face, she carried a riding whip in her hand. In the background was a man dressed in a tuxedo with both hands strapped to a pillory. Across the top was the title song "Revenge, Sweet Revenge" written in dripping, wet blood. I handed it back to her but she gave it to Tull.

"Can I hear a side of this?" he asked Celeste.

"Yeah, take Joe Williams off," Randell shouted. "Let's hear something new. I'm tired of these old classics."

"You tired of Bird." Moose laughed. "Wanna hear something new? Well, put Trane on."

"That old, hippy, sixties music?" Randell laughed. "That's all Trane was."

"You're sick," Moose said. "Trane was a spiritual genius who transcended color, race, everything, man."

"And good music too," Randell said. "Put the album on."

Gussie put the album on and in a few seconds the room was vibrating with a driving punk beat. *Revenge, Sweet Revenge,* the singer bellowed out, *sweeter than the honey in the honeycomb.* Celeste bobbed her head with the beat and swung her hands around like a marionette. Randell listened for a few moments and began to bob his head and snap his fingers too.

Moose screwed up his face and shook his head disdainfully.

"Ah, man, this is a sell-out," he growled. "This is sick! What is Ritual doing this for? This is Nazi music. I liked her better when she was singing jazz."

"Hey, man, let us live, okay," Randell said, but Celeste was too gone into her punk reverie to even bother to care about Moose.

"That's great music," Randell announced to Celeste when the cut was over. "She's a musical genius."

"Trash that anybody'll do to make money," Moose said. "It's a shame that our people are so irresponsible."

"Well, I have to go," Celeste said. "I brought this album by for you," she said to Gussie.

"Are you going to the Mark Taper Forum tonight," he asked Celeste, "for the Media Forum?"

"Oh yes, I heard about that," she said. "Ritual and I were going out to dinner with some friends. What's happenin' there?"

"All the black celebrities are going to be there," Gussie said, "to discuss the problems we're having in the industry."

"Are you going, Celeste?" asked Randell.

"Of course!" she answered. "We'll meet you there after dinner—about ten-thirty?"'

"Good," Randell said. "I liked the album." And Celeste said, "Thank you," just like it was her album.

I told her how glad I was to have seen her and she told me she enjoyed talking to me, even though we hardly had spoken a word to each other, and then she left.

"Ritual is a brilliant singer," Randell said. "She's an innovator."

"She ain't no innovator nothin', asshole"—Moose jumped on him. "You just joining the bandwagon because she got a hit out. Didya see the album cover? That broad was beating men, man? What do you think she's into anyway? She's into perversions! Them white boys like that stuff. Yeah, they be fantasizing about some big black amazon tying them up and beating the shit out of them because of all that guilt they feel from exploiting us. And you, I guess you just like them, huh?"

"You can't blame her because she has a following," Randell said. "She's successful. She's new. Sure, she has a punk crowd behind her but she has a lot of blacks who dig her, too."

"Ah, man you sicker than those sick-ass white boys that want to be beaten. Man, I wished you'd read Marx sometimes and stop being so ignorant!"

"Marx doesn't have anything to do with punk music," Randell said.

"He got everything to do with it," Moose said. "What the fuck do you think he was writing about? What is capitalism but the exploitation of the sexual fantasies of the bourgeoisie?"

"You taking it too serious," Randell said.

"Yeah, and that's why you don't have a job right now. You can't get a job writing in Hollywood because you're black." Moose laughed, and turned to us. "This dude got more degrees than a thermometer and he can't get a job writing a situation comedy about black people because the white boys got it locked down. If this is such a free society, why do the whites write the black shows for blacks? Now, you're a professor of English from Berkeley, tell me how that happened?"

"If the Forum decides to strike, this will be the best thing for the black writer in this town," Randell proclaimed.

"You don't doubt that we will get the strike, do you?" Moose asked.

"No, but I just wonder what really's going to happen if we really did get to do a film. Will we really make it any different?"

Moose stood up, presumably to make a point he couldn't

make sitting down. "Man, you wrote a brilliant script. As soon as the strike closes down *Middle Passage,* we'll hit 'em with your script! Don't worry, we gonna be famous!"

*Middle Passage?* Wasn't that Uncle Gadge's script, I wondered.

Just at that moment, Tull turned to me and asked, "Do you have the car today?"

"Sure," I answered. Once a week I had free use of Mr. Grayeye's Rolls. I did his errands, then took the car back in the evening and picked up my own. He didn't mind, and I liked driving around in it.

"Can you gimme a ride somewhere?" he asked, "It won't take long."

I knew there was more to it than that because when we stepped out onto the balcony he gave me a strange look. As we were cruising down Sunset, I said, "So what's up?"

"These girls wanna meet you . . . doctors' daughters from outa town."

"Where are they," I asked, but he was already pointing ahead to the Dome Restaurant.

"Pull over there," he said, so I swung the Rolls into the entrance, and two carhops popped open the doors for us. I asked Tull to tell me what was happening as we made our way between the tables, but before I could get anything out of him we were standing at the table of these two babes. One was about thirty and pretty ugly, but the younger one was a cutie-pie.

"Sorry I'm late. This is my friend the producer I was tellin' you about," Tull said.

Producer! I could tell right away that Tull had told them a lot of lies, and naturally I felt very uncomfortable. But you shoulda seen the way these "doctors' daughters" jumped all over me. Any idiot could see that they weren't doctors' daughters, just some ordinary floozies trying to get a free ride. During our conversation, the older one, Rosalyn, held a cigarette for me to light and said, "Tull told me you could give us a screen test."

Not knowing how to answer, I said, "Sure," and before I could qualify that, Tull interrupted, "We'll take a ride over to the studio to Jonah's office. Maybe he can take a look at you."

I wanted to strangle that nigger, but I was stuck. So we finished our drinks and went down to the Rolls. When the girls saw that car they almost flipped, but since they were "doctors' daughters" they had to pretend not to be impressed. When we came to the studio gate they nearly croaked at the way the guard waved us on. I took them up to one of the producers' offices, knowing that everyone was gone for the day. I sat behind the desk as if it was mine, and Tull sat on the corner of the desk.

"Walk around a little," I told them. They strolled up and down, switching their asses and giving us stupid looks. It was then that I noticed how really dull they were. Nobody would ever put them in a movie. Finally I stopped them, saying, "I've seen enough. We can't use you."

"But why not?" Rosalyn asked.

I explained, "We are looking for girls from the ghetto, girls that can cuss and don't mind playing hip prostitutes. But you're doctors' daughters. You have too much class." They gave each other a look and Rosalyn went over to whisper into the other one's ear.

Finally, she came over to us. "Hey, baby, we hip. We are really working girls. Linda works for the telephone company and I am a nurse. We can play the kind of girls you' lookin' for."

Acting surprised, I said, "But I thought you were daughters of doctors from out of town?"

"No, we just made that up," Linda said, speaking for practically the first time since we came into the studio.

Tull stood up and looked at his watch. "Look you've taken

up enough of this man's time. He is very busy. He has to get to an important meeting at the Mark Taper Forum."

"That's right," I said, thinking of Gussie and the Media Forum. "I have to leave."

Nobody spoke as we drove the girls to the ghetto where they proudly told us they lived. When we opened the door for them, they pleaded with us to come up to see how they live, and said that perhaps we could use their apartment for a scene in the movie.

"It's very realistic," Rosalyn said, but I said we really had to go.

"Please come by anytime," Linda said, "and let us entertain you."

"We will," Tull answered.

"Promise?" they called as we pulled off.

Once away from there Tull and I had a big laugh, but I made him promise never to do that to me again. He claimed he wouldn't, but I didn't believe him. I returned Mr. Grayeye's Rolls and picked up my own car from the studio, and when we got back to the Fountain Lanai we knocked on Gussie's door.

"Hey, let's be getting over to the Forum!" Gussie said, looking at his watch. Then we piled into Gussie's BMW and headed for downtown Los Angeles.

# 12

B UT when we got to the corner of Santa Monica and
Fairfax, Gussie spied Janet. "Look at her," he said and
he pointed to a woman in a red bikini dancing in front of a
bus-stop bench on the corner. Clad only in this red bathing
suit and a sailor's cap, Janet did a bump and grind to the
beat of the radio on her shoulder. People stopped, stared,
shook their heads, and motored on; most just ignored her.

"Look at that," Gussie said. "If the Hudsons saw that,
they'd pack up and leave. Isn't she disgusting?"

I asked if she were a prostitute.

"Naw, she just flips out every now and then. She use to be
an actress. Beautiful woman. She use to be in those old
movies but she can't get work anymore, and she can't face
the fact that she's a failure. So she has a nervous breakdown
every few weeks and goes out to various parts of the city and
does just what you see her doing now. Pull over to the curb,
Tull, I want to give her another warning."

Tull pulled over to the corner. Old Janet was going at it.
She was dancing and rolling her behind and laughing at the
world as it turned.

"Janet. Listen, I don't want you coming back into the
Fountain Lanai. Janet, pack it in, sweetheart. You are
finished in this town, Janet."

She didn't even notice us. She just kept on dancing and
acting crazy.

"Leave her alone," Randell said. "Let her live."

Tull pulled off and left her. Gussie swore that he was kicking her out the first thing in the morning.

The Mark Taper Forum auditorium was crowded. Over five hundred black people crammed the space. Blacks from the most revolutionary and radical media groups sat in the back. Those with the most accommodating attitude toward the white powers-that-be sat up front, just a little to the right of the speaker's lectern.

We—Gussie, Moose, Randell, Tull, and me—sat down among some rough-looking street blacks way over in the back. As I got comfortable in my seat I looked over into the section of the black celebrities, which was down close to the stage to the right. I looked for my uncle and Aunt Lottie among the faces of celebrities like Sidney Poitier, Brock Peters, and Cicely Tyson. Everybody was looking at this section to see who was there. Then I saw them. My uncle sat in the front row as if he were in heaven waiting for St. Peter to warm up the Sermon on the Mount for Moses. I could see the light reflect on the light bald spot on his forehead. Under the dark-blue Roos Atkin's necktie his stomach rose and fell with the rapt, attentive rhythm of anticipation of some future success. His face exuded a pompous arrogance. His golden watchband, picking up the floodlights, exuded power and confidence. Even his ten fingers—each one manicured and filed to just the right length at an expensive shop— connoted success. When the discussion began after the main speech, Uncle Gadge joined the panel on the stage.

As the wife of a successful man, Aunt Lottie complemented him so thoroughly that they would have been a perfect center-page fold-out for Werner Erhard's *est Graduate* review.

MC Jim Avalone peacocked to the microphone.

"Ladies and Gents," he said, "the Black Media Forum has a distinguished guest tonight who will never let us down. Let black Hollywood give a great big hand to a great big friend in the great big White House! Mr. Andrew Jackson from the F.C.C."

A white man with a full head of the whitest hair I had ever seen, bearing a suspicious resemblance to ex-candidate John Anderson, took command of the microphone. I wondered if he must be feeling a little nervous—though he didn't look anything less than cool as a cucumber—to be practically the only white man in the room, looking out at this sea of black faces, most of them angry. But he seemed to be on familiar and even friendly terms with many of the front row of celebrity blacks, who were all sitting up with rapt attention like this was church or something, and he was the visiting preacher about to give the Sunday sermon.

"Things are bad for black people in Hollywood," he said, right off in a the-way-things-are tone of voice. Heads nodded and a few "That's right's" and "Uh-huh's" leaped into the air.

"They are bad because from the very beginning of the movie industry, blacks were given a sorry role. Hollywood, more than any other institution, helped to perpetuate racial bias by retaining a *tradition* of demeaning blacks! It started with blackface, when black people weren't even allowed to portray themselves in films, and white actors put cork on their faces and rendered derogatory caricatures of the Negro race. Al Jolson, Shirley Temple, Judy Garland, and countless other white stars used blackface in films."

He went on to describe how stereotypes were perpetuated, using black actors and actresses in the roles. Hattie McDaniels, the mammy in *Gone with the Wind,* Butterfly McQueen, and the shiftless servant Stepin Fetchit in many films. To find the answer to the problems of stereotypes we must go back to slavery, he told us.

How was he going to tie slavery into this? First, he started telling us about the slave ships. Right on the front rows right up there where the expensive seats were, you could see the Negro lawyers and doctors and famous actors with their wives in furs and diamond rings begin bobbing their heads obsequiously and taking in all this crap.

The fact that slavery had nothing to do with films didn't stop old knucklehead Jackson, though. He tied it in somehow. He tied it in with *The Birth of a Nation* because, he said, as if we didn't already know it, this was the first racist film. Then, he went on to talk in detail about *Gone with the Wind* and what a horrible film that was for blacks. He went on to tie it in with Hattie McDaniels and how when people complained that she had played a maid in that film, she said, she'd rather be a maid in a film than a maid in life. You should've seen the bourgeois heads bobbing up and down then! Tears were practically rolling down their cheeks. Amens were floating up from these noble faces. It's incredible how much phoney stuff black people will take if a white man in a position of authority dishes it out to them.

In winding up his speech, Mr. Jackson cited a few films like *Sounder, Roots,* and *Plantation* (Uncle Gadge's film) as signs that there had been "some progress" made. These films, he said, had "reconciled the difference between the races." And let us hope, he went on, that more films like these will help to keep "harmony between the races." The function of the F.C.C., he said, was to preserve this "diversity."

As soon as he sat down, my Uncle Gadge and the other celebrities shot to their feet and gave him a standing ovation.

The majority of the five hundred blacks, however, sat silent, conspicuously unimpressed.

"The house is opened for questions," MC Avelone announced.

A deadly silence swallowed up the room again.

A large black sister raised her hand.

"Yes, sister?" the MC said, and everybody turned to see who the person to ask the first question was.

"I have just witnessed a miracle," the large heavyset sister in a red pants suit said. "I come here from the ghetto to hear this man talk about the racism against black people. But all he talked about was how bad things is. It was a nice speech. I felt sorry for myself, but what did it have to do about these stereotypes on TV? I have two teenagers and I don't want them watching these negative black images on *Good Times* and the *Jeffersons*. I don't! How can we get more blacks jobs in the media? He didn't say anything about that. All he said was the same old bullshit. I think we oughta boycott these damn television producers. And hurt them in their pocketbooks. We oughta do it now. We ought to get up off our lazy asses and . . ."

". . . Sister," The MC interposed. "Sister . . . !"

". . . do something about it. . . . We oughta put some fire . . ."

". . . Right on!" somebody next to her shouted. *"Preach!"*

". . . under the asses of these big-shot black Hollywood stars and make them . . ."

". . . *Sister,"* the MC went on, his voice rising louder to drown her out, ". . . We want only questions, not *statements!"*

"LET HER TALK!" a boisterous voice shouted at the MC from the sea of black faces.

". . . I'll be forced to shut you off," Avelone warned.

"Right on, sister!" somebody else shouted. "I agree with her!"

"Yeah! Boycott the producers!"

"We WANNA VOTE ON IT!"

The blacks began shouting and clamoring and hooting. Finally, when the MC got them quieted down, he asked the black panel behind him on stage, "Well, anybody on our panel like to answer this question?"

Uncle Gadge rose from his seat and raised his hand.

"We have the screenwriter Gadge Drinkwater, who is going to answer your question," he said. "Just be patient now."

Gadge took the microphone and faced the floodlights with a fixed-on grin.

"I don't think violence solves anything," Uncle began, even though nobody had mentioned violence. "We should look to *art* for our inspiration! The artist must have artistic freedom. By voting for a strike we are doing merely what the powers-that-be want! I agree with our distinguished guest speaker! It is excellence we must seek! And those great names of literature and art—those names of Lorraine Hansberry and Langston Hughes and Paul Robeson—will look down from Olympus and smile on us. In the immortal words of the poet laureate of Harlem, Hideho Heights, who wrote, 'The present is only intelligible in the light of the past,' I gladly thank Mr. Andrew Jackson for taking out the time from his busy schedule to come share with us some of his great wisdom."

He ended his speech, and all of those who agreed with him began to applaud him as he sat down. The rest of us sat silently. There were murmurs of disapproval rising from the audience. It was too obvious that my uncle had delivered a speech for the benefit of the white bourgeoisie. Even the whites felt that and a few began to squirm in their seats as the blacks began to mutter louder their displeasure. My uncle reared way back in his seat and held Aunt Lottie's hand tightly while the whites nearly broke their necks trying to get over to him to thank him for that speech.

The chair then recognized the next speaker. I was surprised when Moose, who was sitting next to me, rose.

When the audience turned to look, what they saw was this huge black giant. He was the nigger that every white feared. His long, dyed locks fled in various directions, like the snakes on Medusa's head. His skin was coal black, his voice the unmistakable echo of some tragic injustice. Moose was articulate. He was an educated black man, one of their own sons; his life had begun as a symbol of hope. He had gone to college, had a good heart, but he still was a victim of injustice. He was from the sixties. He was angry, very angry.

"We heard the speech of the distinguished speaker. It's a paean to Uncle Tomism. Maybe Uncle Tom is gone but now we have to keep an eye on Dr. *Thomas*. We support the strike. The masses of blacks are exploited by the few. It doesn't matter if the few are black or white. Is that what you mean by 'harmony between the races'? Then the blacks and whites should get together and boycott the few that are creating negative stereotypes of us. We should boycott Democracy for its slave pictures. We don't want any more *Roots, Middle Passages,* or *any* plantation films. Give us films where the blacks *revolt* on the plantation and throw over the oppressive masters. Yeah! We don't wanna hear this bullshit about 'Art' because you bourgeois Uncle Toms don't know anything about art. By art you mean 'materialism.' We're tired of rousing up the conscience of the people only to have the few white-blacks reap all the benefits just because the conscience of the whites is guilty. Down with Uncle Tomism and up with revolt! We must fight to get what we want! And we must organize an immediate strike against Democracy *now!*"

When he was finished, the blacks applauded him.

The MC came back. "Ladies and Gents. We will now hear from Yolanda Nkomo Saba from the Black Women's Committee."

Yolanda rose. A creole co-ed, she looked like a young actress in search of the perfect script. Her short, neat natural emphasized her pure African features. She wore an African caftan of green and gold and spoke in a clear, sonorous, Southern accent.

"We have heard both sides expressed this evening, but

none of them express the problem of the black woman. When you men argue about the plight of the actor or the writer in this business, you are thinking of the male, whether he is the black who is oppressed, or the white who oppresses. Women suffer the worst from these plantation films, because it is the men who draw up these fantasies about women. This is the real source of the stereotypes. In this slave picture, *Middle Passage,* atrocities are committed against white women as well as the blacks. Despite the Scarlett O'Hara similarity, the heroine of this film is nothing more than a prostitute. Three of these characters are lesbians. One particularly deplorable case of homosexual love between a young black slave girl and her white mistress is totally unnecessary. Not to mention the assorted mammas and mulatto wenches.

"Yet even in their degradation white women are given more respect than black women," she said.

"Right on!" a black woman cheered.

"For example, in the script of the film, when the white woman is raped by the black slave, she is given three pages in which she expresses her feelings on being raped. In fact, when she finishes her speech, you wonder if the writer didn't invent the incident in order to give the white actress a bigger part. While when the black slave girl is raped by her master, which appears on page 92, she is given only this line, *'T'se always loves you, sir!'* "

Everybody laughed at that, even some of the bourgeoisie.

"Neither of these groups speak for us women," Yolanda said. "The strike would not help us. How can it? When the demands are won, it will be the men who profit from it."

Uncle Gadge started smiling and nodded his head, as did the others who didn't want the strike.

"Yet we feel that we should not vote against any strike

that seeks to correct the ills of this media community. Therefore we, as part of a large community, are casting our sympathy *for the strike!*"

The auditorium went wild. The session was adjourned. The doors flew open and the crowd spread out onto the plaza.

# 13

As we were standing outside on the plaza watching the people, a lady came up to us and said she was Brenda Whitehead from KIXN News and asked if she could interview Moose.

Moose looked at Randell for approval. "Should I?"

"Yeah, go ahead."

"And then what?" Moose asked.

"Just rap," Randell said coolly.

Moose turned to Brenda Whitehead. "What do you want to know?"

"Well, let's start with your background?" she said, sticking a microphone up into his mouth.

Looking at the mike, Moose snickered. "Okay. I grew up in the sixties. I was a young black male searching for his manhood. I read Fanon's *Wretched of the Earth* and Al Fatah's *The Revolution and Violence, The Road to Victory,* Bakunin's *Catechism of a Revolutionist,* and Eldridge's *Soul on Ice,* and I *heard* Stokely Carmichael's June 1966 speech in which he said, and I quote, 'The only way we gonna stop them white men from whuppin' us is to take over. We been saying freedom for six years and we ain't got nothin', what we gonna start saying now is Black Power.' When I heard H. Rap Brown say, 'Burn, baby, burn'; when I saw brothers go from Molotov cocktails to dynamite, heard Radio Free Dixie, and heard Robert Williams of the Revolutionary American Movement; and heard Aimé Césaire on 'Negritude,' heard Fanon on the rhapsodic transformation of the colonized 'object' into a person of dignity through violence; when I heard brother Eldridge say, 'Violence alone makes it possible for the masses to understand social truths and give the key to them.' When I read these authors and understood them, I became a man. An American. A true American. When you have known freedom it's very hard to accept bullshit."

She stuck the mike into her own mouth and said, "Are you here to attack black Hollywood?"

"We here to stand up," Moose said. "It's absurd to think we are going to attack Hollywood just because we are against black stereotypes!"

Brenda Whitehead put the mike over to Randell and asked him what he thought, but he wouldn't say anything.

Moose went on, though. "This is the American tradition. Every nation that has won its independence has done it through violence. Even Israel. Especially Israel. June 18, 1946, for example. The Irgun, the Israeli terrorist group, kidnapped five British officers in Tel Aviv and held them hostage," Moose said.

Everybody was impressed by his facts! He's smart! A bit off his rocker, all right! But he knew what he was talking about. It was funny. That Brenda was very funny. She wanted to cut him off but everybody standing around was fascinated with this incredible-looking person. A famous black movie star stood and gaped with interest.

"The Israeli terrorists held them hostage and in July 22 of the same year at the King David Hotel this same group of terrorists killed ninety British in a bombing. What happened as a result of this? The British granted amnesty to the resistance members and the land became the state of Israel. Therefore we must fight the tyranny in Hollywood just as the Irgun and LEHI Israeli terrorists fought in 1946. Fight against the sexual insults against women and the racial insults against blacks. We have to terrorize the studios until they give up their tyranny over our feelings."

A black woman standing behind him applauded him. Then everybody else clapped him.

"How can we take what you say seriously?" Brenda said. "After all," she said, "by your own admission, you're a terrorist."

I didn't realize how crowded the Forum had been until I went downstairs to take a leak. Even the entrance to the men's room was packed with celebrities. There was nothing impressive about these guys when you saw them down there looking uncomfortable.

Inside the bathroom, Uncle Gadge was talking to a balding man in his fifties. I heard somebody say he was the artistic director of the Mark Taper Forum.

I took a leak right beside them.

"I'm not interested in politics," Gadge was going on excitedly. "Art is art. I want you to give me enough space to get a couple run-throughs. Can you do that?"

"Absolutely, Gadge," the man said, shaking his wee-wee over the urinal. "We'll have the space to put on your play anytime. I loved your *Black Christ*."

They went out. It wasn't that Gadge hadn't seen me—he had. He would never speak to me in situations like this because he was actually talking that guy into a business deal to get his play on. You gotta admire Gadge. He knows how to use liberals and he's always blowing his horn.

As I was coming out of the building onto the plaza again, I spied Gadge standing on the sidewalk with the balding man between two cars. Gadge was giving him a one and one of cocaine.

When I got back, a television crew was now taping a live interview with Moose. I stood in the crowd listening to him for a moment. Then I saw Randell was rapping to Celeste and a beautiful woman I took to be the famous Ritual Bondage. Now, I love celebrities like everybody else. So I hustled over to where this woman was clad in this multi-colored boa of feathers.

"Hello," I said to Celeste, and she introduced me to her.

She had a thin, slender physique. Her big black eyes spoke of sensuality and understanding. There was something repulsive yet fascinating in her face. I was both attracted and repelled by her large sensual mouth, her flaring nostrils, and her insouciant, musical voice.

But it wasn't me she noticed. It was Randell Young.

"It's such a pleasure to meet you," she said to him.

"Randell is a writer," Celeste said. "He wrote the movie *Let's Get Down!*"

"I love your work," she said to him.

"I really love your work," Randell said.

Just then Yolanda came up behind Randell and threw her arms around him playfully.

Randell threw her into his arms. "You gave a wonderful speech." He laughed. "Thanks for saving us!"

She hugged him again.

"Isn't it wonderful? We're finally going to make a change in this town!"

Yolanda had come with a white man about twenty-five. Now he stood behind her, embarrassed. She turned to him and introduced him to us.

"This is my husband," she said, "Mark. Mark, this is the brilliant brother who is a terrific novelist, and screenwriter. My husband is a producer."

Randell's face dropped when she said he was her husband but he shook the guy's hand and turned to Ritual. "This is Ritual Bondage," Randell said to Yolanda.

"It's very important for me to shake your hand," Yolanda said. "I've always admired your music."

"Thank you," Ritual said. "You gave a very noble, moving speech! I want you to know that I support what you said, and if I can help you on the strike, please let me know."

"Thank you so much," Yolanda said, again.

Randell said, "Yolanda is right up there with the big wheels over at Tandem Productions, where they do all those funny kinda black situation comedies like *Good Times, The Jeffersons,* and *Diff'rent Strokes.*"

"Yeah? Looks like something good for you, huh?" Ritual said, suddenly giving Randell all of her attention, though people were practically standing in line to talk to her.

"Excuse us! Television crew coming through!"

The television crew pushed everybody aside except Randell. As the camera isolated him, Brenda moved in on him with the microphone. "Can you give us a concise statement about tonight's event?" she asked Randell.

"There is a new revolution afoot in black cinema," he said, and turned to Ritual.

"Thank you very much, Randell Young. This is KIXN News," she said into the camera.

While everybody was laughing, Ritual pulled Randell's coat and whispered to him, "We're going to my place for drinks."

"Outa sight," Randell said. "Let's go!"

Ritual had a limousine and we—Celeste, me, Randell, and Gussie—piled in and took off.

# 14

THE limousine made an arc on Sunset and glided to a squat in front of the Sunset Tower, that monument to 1930's Hollywood where Ritual had told us she lived. She had pointed it out to us so that we could presumably appreciate it in its context. Tall, elegant, unique, white, aristocratic, she reared up with dignity against the Hollywood Hills that could boast that they were the favorite home of the glittering stars.

A doorman in white gloves opened the limousine door. On our way into the lobby, a pair of plaster Greek nymphs greeted us with painted-on smiles. While we waited for the elevator, a bouquet of beautiful flowers passed us on its way to congratulate, woo, or console somebody. Then the elevator gaped its mouth and vomited out a punk with a red crew cut and a radio blaring Ritual's hit.

"Hey, that's your song!" Randell said. Ritual smiled back at him.

"Well, what can I say? I have a hit." She laughed and we joined in with her.

We stepped off the cloud at the ninth floor and Ritual sesamed the door to her apartment and we stepped off into her heaven.

"This is my place," she announced and what a place it was. Panoramic view of the city, like breathtaking. It felt like you were in a jetliner hovering over a city at night. Just before the plane landed, you could see the city lights against the black velvety darkness like glittering diamonds. I stood there looking at it. You could see the city lights as far as the Los Angeles Airport, and right next door in the other apartment you see a woman walking around in her underwear; they had their Esmeraldas just as we did.

"Let me show you around," Ritual said and took Randell by the arm and took him into the next room. I followed. She showed us a room that looked like Jean Harlow's boudoir. Then the bedroom: the walls in pink satin, the bed set behind curtains like a stage. Then the automatic controls that made it rise and fall or massage you to sleep. Celeste asked her to push the button that pushed back a door that hid all of her hundreds of pairs of shoes and dresses. But no, she wasn't out to impress anybody and she refused, laughing.

Satisfied that we were seated comfortably on the sofa in the living room, Ritual went into the kitchen to get some champagne, and Celeste went to help her.

"Put on any record you like," Ritual yelled from the kitchen. I went to the ample record collection and began to look through them. Most of the records were by Ritual, and I pulled out an old record she must've done many years ago. Her name wasn't really Ritual Bondage, I realized when I looked at an album that featured her as Gertrude Williams —*Gertrude Williams Sings Jazz*. There were listed such classic numbers as "My Lover Man," "Nobody Knows You When You're Down and Out." The girl on the jacket was no more than twenty-one. She had a Dionne Warwick-like face. High cheekbones. One hundred percent Negro. Almond-shaped eyes. Flared nostrils, wide minstrelsy lips.

"Can we hear this?" I asked when she returned with the champagne.

"That one?" she laughed, and she took the record and went to the turntable.

"Let me see that?" Randell asked, and I gave him the picture of her. "Gertrude Williams." He laughed. "I like your real name better."

Ritual turned from the machine. "You do? Much better than Ritual? I do too," she confessed with a laugh. "But after the success of that record *Ritual Bondage,* people started calling me that. I don't know if you know this, but we singers have to yield to the public."

"I quite understand," Randell said.

"Do you? I wouldn't want you to misunderstand," she laughed. "I hear writers are very sensitive. So what will you call me? Ritual or Gertrude?"

They shared a laugh.

"I like Gertrude," Randell said. "Trudy—that's what I'll call you."

Ritual vibrated with laughter like loose rose petals in a thunderstorm. "Oh, that's just fine with me," she said, raising her glass. We all followed our hostess's suit. "To my new name—Trudy!"

Laughing, we toasted her. The champagne was cold and delicious.

"Oh, I love this song. You really sing jazz beautifully," Randell exclaimed.

"Thank you. It's my first love," Gertrude went on. "But jazz singers starve in this town. I have to sing disco, and when that plays out, I have to go on to punk. I hate apologizing like this, but for some reason I feel I want to with you."

"Oh, don't feel that way," Randell said. "We all have to make compromises."

Celeste interposed another subject of conversation. "What did you think of the speaker at the Forum, Mr. Andrew Jackson?" she asked Randell.

"I can only say he must have had a lot of help from a black person." Randell laughed. "I was really impressed that he knew so much about black history."

"I was, too," Gertrude said. "He seemed very informed about us."

"Too informed," Tull said, laughing. "He didn't leave anything for us to complain about it."

"Yeah," I said, "it was as though he was expressing our complaints for us."

"Well, it's become a cliché now for whites to take up our protest for us!" Randell said. "It use to be that we could complain about how bad race prejudice is. Now the whites have become sophisticated. Like this speaker tonight, he was out to appease the mass of us by conjuring up all the stereotypes. I noticed that these stereotypes still had the power to hurt black people. Every time the speaker said something about Uncle Toms or Mammas or Stepin Fetchit, we shouted 'Right on!' but we forgot that he was using them in exactly the same way as the whites used them in the films—to shock us, to get an emotional response from us. These stereotypes, therefore, as far as I'm concerned, are not meaningless. We are still emotionally involved with them."

"This is true," Gertrude said, sipping her champagne and nodding at Randell. "When I first started singing, the producers didn't know what to do with me. I had no image. I was just some young black chick who had a good voice, but they hadn't found an 'image' for me. First they tried me as the young 'Odetta-type,' but that didn't stick with the public. Then, they tried the 'soul sister' image and that didn't work. Finally, they dressed me in this expensive leopard outfit and started giving me songs about how mean I could be to men, and that image stuck with the public. I became the black erotic Tigress, the Temptress. Like Josephine Baker. I had to appear on one jacket cover nude except for a pink flamingo feather!"

Randell seemed embarrassed.

"That's wonderful," he exclaimed. "You're so beautiful! Then you're not fooled by all this image, are you?"

"Of course not," she shouted. "I'm not at all like that cover has me," she said, pointing to the Ritual Bondage album lying on the glass-top table before us.

"That's very true," Randell said.

"How would everybody like to try something different?" Gertrude asked us. Then she looked at Randell dubiously. "I guess you've never tried freebase?" she asked.

"No, what is it?" he asked.

"I cooked up some," Trudy said. "I'll bring it out and we can try it together."

I watched her bring in some white crystal on a transparent plate.

"This is the cocaine," she said, explaining the white crystal on the plate. She took a razor blade and scraped the crystal off the plate and placed it on the top of a water pipe. Then she took the pipe in her mouth and lit a cigarette lighter to the crystal. We watched curiously as the lighter's flame melted the white crystal. A fist of white smoke cloud opened its fingers in the bottom of the glass pipe. Trudy took a deep breath, pulling the smoke out of the pipe and into her lungs. She passed the pipe to Celeste and held her breath. Celeste with a quick gesture placed the pipe in ready position. "Let it cool," she said.

We watched Trudy. She held back her head, closed her eyes, as if she were in a trance. She sucked in the air, and held it.

Then I deciphered the secret meaning behind her record-jacket pictures. Pictures of the Temptress. Pictures of a trance-induced soothsayer witch, voodoo queen!

She may have been right about the "image" of being a sex symbol—just a symbol—but I didn't believe her. What I believed was that she wanted Randell to think she was just as innocent as a newborn baby. What she wanted, I decided, was to get him to fall in love with her. This was what she must have done many times before. Randell was so unsuspecting that he was already practically eating out of her hand.

Gradually, she allowed the air to escape from her lungs, her eyes bucked and then began to close until they were barely opened. Sloe-eyed, I believe they call it. Sexy-eyed. Whatever they call it, it all means the same thing—horny. Just like she is on the jacket cover of her records.

"How was it?" Celeste asked.

"Fantastic!" she said. "That was a good hit," she said in a faraway voice.

Then she picked up the pipe again and refilled it and offered it to old Randell. Randell made a gesture that revealed he didn't want to be a square. There was a look on Gertrude's face that said she wanted him to accept her because if he didn't accept her she would be embarrassed around him.

"Do you want to do this?" she asked him as she offered the pipe to him.

"Of course," he said. "Thank you."

Gertrude smiled with relief and like a mother instructing a child began to show him how to do it.

"First, relax. Now gradually inhale. Not too fast. That's right. Slow and easy. Good—that's good," she said, and took the pipe out of his mouth. "Now hold it in. Good. Now gradually let it out of your lungs." And as old Randell did that, she stroked him verbally: "Very, very good!"

I was next. She scraped some of the flaky, milk-colored cocaine off the plate with a razor blade and placed it on the little screen on the pipe. Then she put the blazing pencil-thin tongue of the butane burner onto the coke, which dissolved instantly.

"Now draw easy," she instructed me while I smelled the expensive perfume of her body and saw the diamond rings on her finger. "Easy now, that's good. Draw it all down and hold it!"

138 |

Tull and Celeste were next. But my own feelings took up all of my consciousness; I flipped out. A euphoric feeling swept me like a wave in the sea. The room swayed back and forth comfortably, filling me with a strong feeling of control.

"That's good," Randell said. "You're right. We must use our stereotypes to make a living."

"Yes, that's right!" Gertrude said. "That's our only way out of this trap!"

"The white world has made freaks of us," Celeste said, "and now we must accept the roles of freaks!"

"We are like somebody trapped in a nightmare," Tull said.

"Does anybody want another hit?" Gertrude asked, offering the pipe.

"I'll have another one," Randell said. After the hit, he said, "That's good! Yes, everybody is right. We are in an ironical situation. We are black in the Great White World. We can only make money by being what they want us to be."

I couldn't believe what we were doing, talking out of our minds! Didn't they see the ironical situation? As Randell had put it, here we were the most talented of our race and all we were doing was destroying our minds! I began to hallucinate. I saw Gertrude as a big eagle with razor-sharp talons. She hovered over Randell, who was a little rabbit with a white tail, wearing glasses. The eagle swooped down on the rabbit and caught him in her talons and flew away in the sky. I was screaming at the eagle, "No!" I must've said it aloud because Tull turned to me and said, "No what?"

"Oh, no nothing!"

"Have you ever noticed that any honesty is greeted by laughter in this town," Randell said, more to the enchanting hostess than to us. "This is an axiom. If you tell somebody something truly honest, they react with laughter here. The worst things are done with laughter."

I wanted to see if that was true. I thought I'd try it on the stage. I looked at my watch. It would still be time enough for me to go on the stage.

I looked around and Randell and Gertrude were dancing. The music was bouncing off the walls, and the next thing I knew I was dancing, too.

I've got to get out of here, I decided, and went out the door. I don't think anybody even cared that I'd left. When I got down to the lobby I was surprised to discover Tull standing beside me.

"I had to come see about you," he said. "You just suddenly bolted for the door. Are you okay?"

"Yeah, I think so," I said, but I was hallucinating. I kept seeing monsters walking down Sunset.

"Come on," he said. "I'll walk you home. It's not far."

"No, I want to go to the Comedy Club," I said, pointing to the neon sign right up the street. "I want to go on the stage. I want to see if what Randell said is true. You know what he said? In Hollywood the truth is embarrassing. Everybody responds to the truth with laughter. Is he right? I'm in the mood to tell them the truth tonight."

"You're too high, man."

"That's just the state you have to be in to tell the truth. Come on."

Following me up to the Comedy Club, Tull was dubious. He kept telling me that I was too high to go on stage.

"I've got to try everything until I find myself," I told him, when we were within a few steps of the club.

"Find yourself? What do you mean?"

I had never explained it to anybody before. "You know? Stage presence. Image, just what Randell and Gertrude were talking about. I don't have it yet. I have these jokes but I don't have humor. I want to have everything I say come out of me. I've got to find my own style. I'm fed up with waiting, too."

"Yeah, but you seem pretty funny to me!"

"That's because I'm your friend."

The club was crowded. I decided that I'd be honest with everybody I saw that evening. I wouldn't pretend, as I knew was expected of me. No social pretenses. When I saw Thalia, she had on an absolutely horrible, oversized, overexpensive dress.

"Do you like it?" she asked. "The dress?"

"You look like a bitch who just spent too much money on a dress," I joked—ha, ha, ha!—bursting out into a hyena's laugh. I felt embarrassed, but Randell was right. She covered her embarrassment with laughter. When the MC came down she told him to let me go on next.

I sat down with Tull with a drink until the comic was finished. The MC introduced me. I went up there.

"Good evening? There's nothing good about this evening. I'm loaded and fucked up," I said. "And you are fucked up too? Aren't you?"

They belly-laughed.

"You are a bunch of assholes to come out here to this club to see me. Really, because I'm not going to tell you any jokes tonight. I'm going to be just honest with you."

The silence opened its yawning mouth and waited.

Would I deliver? Could I deliver? Suddenly my anger and bitterness gave way and I started to laugh at my own self. I didn't understand anymore why I'd said what I'd said. Here was the moment that I had been waiting for. They were waiting for me to give them the truth.

Suddenly the moment was past. It was all over with. I felt it, and started telling them jokes from my own routine. I got the same applause I'd gotten before, but it wasn't what I'd been trying to get at. When I came down the aisle, a few people thanked me, but I knew I had been mediocre.

"You were great," Tull said, but I knew he just said it to

make me feel good. No, he didn't see what I had in mind. Nobody did. I hadn't found myself and I felt even more frustrated as I walked down Fountain to our apartment. I felt empty and depressed for attempting it. I wanted to be free, to find myself.

"I tried. I was almost there. Didn't you see how they were opened to me, but then I let them off. I let them go!"

"I see what you're talking about," Tull said. "I think." We came to the apartment building.

"Well, what do you think of Ritual?" he asked me with a laugh.

"I've never met anybody like her," I told him my honest feelings. "She's a superstar."

"She has a very strange reputation in this town," Tull said. "She traps men like a black-widow spider. But Randell seems to be different."

We came to Lanai and walked through the gate to the patio.

"Where did Randell come from?" I asked as we passed the swimming pool.

"Him and Moose came here about six months ago from San Francisco. Randell was teaching at Berkeley but Moose, I think, had just got out of jail. They had decided back ten years ago to come to Hollywood one day and be famous. That's what Randell told me. But, man, that's more than a notion in this town."

We went up to our apartment and just as Tull put his key in the lock a blood-curdling scream came from one of the other apartments.

"Sounds like somebody being murdered!" I exclaimed.

"Ah, that ain't nobody but them lesbians up there." And he pointed to the apartment above Gussie's. The light was on but the shade was partially drawn. I saw two silhouettes struggling. I could make out two slender figures tussling with each other.

142 |

"They do that every weekend. One of them finds out that the other one has screwed some guy and they get into a brawl about it," he said, opening the door and going in.

"You coming in?" he asked. I was standing on the balcony. What I was doing, I was trying to see if any of the other perverts were up. Old Janet's light was out.

"Naw, I'm going to smoke a cigarette out here," I told him. "You go ahead. I'll be in later."

He closed the door and I lighted up a cigarette. The building was very quiet, with the exception of the lesbians, and they quieted down after a bit. From Steve's apartment I heard the whining of hard rock music. What an evening this had been! I kept thinking about the Media Forum and about Uncle Gadge and Moose. I was surprised at the way black people were so media-conscious and at how easily manipulated they were by people like my uncle. But I was excited and pleased with my new roommate and all the assorted people who lived in the complex. I was drawn to Randell as if he were somebody I'd known all my life. I remembered my Uncle Lindsey and I thought that he and Randell were very much alike. I thought of Moose. I could easily understand him, too. He was not afraid to tell white people how angry he was. I liked that very much. I kept thinking how attractive Randell was to Ritual and I felt embarrassment. She seemed so much different from him. She was a famous superstar and he was a mere writer. Could they be happy together? Did people often fall in love in Hollywood in one night? Or was this an exception to the rule?

I put my cigarette out and walked out of the Fountain Lanai. I walked down Fountain to Santa Monica, where the cluster of brightly lighted shopping center and stores were. Gays strolled along under the lights, swishing their behinds at the cars and their cruising passengers. I kept thinking about the future of the Black Media Forum. Was there going to be a boycott of Democracy? Or was this as far as it would go? Everything was so new to me that I was excited over the possibility of something interesting happening. Anyway, whatever happened, I'd get material from it for my act. I headed back for the Lanai.

# 15

WHEN I came back into the courtyard I heard the clacking of typewriter keys coming from Randell's apartment. As I drew closer I saw the dude himself all bent over his machine. It must've been about four in the morning. I knocked on the door and he said come in. I went in. Randell was seated at the typewriter and he didn't look up. Balls of paper festooned the trash basket at the side of the desk. Above his head was a large map that had been drawn in a crudely artistic hand.

"Want some coffee?" he asked, still not looking up. "Go ahead. It's in the kitchen. I'll be with you in a minute." I went into the kitchen, poured myself some coffee, while he tapped away like a madman. There was a large poster of John Coltrane with a train superimposed over it. This was probably Moose's side of the room. On the other side of the room, where Randell sat, there was a poster of Charlie Parker and superimposed over it was a bird. Bird and Trane. On Randell's side were books by Ionesco, Poe, Twain, Alexander Dumas, Camus, Faulkner, Himes, Baudelaire. On Moose's side of the room were books by Eldridge Cleaver, George Jackson, the Marquis de Sade, and the Prison writings of Soviet Dissidents. Then I saw a batch of screenplays. When Randell saw me pick up a batch of screenplays, he leaned back in the wooden straight chair.

"Most white guys write one screenplay as an example of their abilities." He laughed. "I wrote six!"

"Why did you write so many?"

"Producers are finicky when it comes to us black writers. A white guy can demonstrate his form, but we have to have screenplays on various subjects. You know, black writers are identified with *content;* white writers with form."

"When did you write all these?"

"When I was teaching English at Berkeley," he said. "Then I quit and came to Hollywood to make it."

"Say, what'd you think of that Ritual babe?" I sort of wanted to tease him about her.

Pushing his glasses back on his face with an unconscious gesture, he nodded and a smile blossomed on his lips. "Wonderful woman," he said. "So talented. When I hear her sing, I want to cry. She's a symbol for me of all black women, their ugliness and their beauty all in one."

"She sort of dug you, huh?"

"Man, I hope so. 'Cause I *dug* her."

"So what 'ya gonna do? Get married or what? Take her out and stuff?"

"We'll see," he said, standing up. "But, you know, she's exploited just like the rest of the blacks in Hollywood. You know these record companies treat these black disco singers just like they are whores. At best, expensive courtesans."

"She told you all this?"

"She doesn't have to tell me," he said, padding to the coffeepot across the room. "I've been in this evil fucking town long enough to know how these goddamn vultures treat black talent. These assholes! This woman has a great gift, and they exploit her!"

I pointed out to him that she didn't seem to be complaining, and that she really seemed very well taken care of, considering where she lived and how laid out her apartment was.

"She's broke," he said, pouring some coffee now.

"Broke?"

146

"You know what these record companies do, don't you?" he asked, looking at me over the coffee cup, "These record company guys are the worst. Slave masters, jack. They take all of her money, pay her bills, she never has her own capital to invest. They take all of it for their fees. They treat her like she's their whore. I tell you! I know this town."

"Do you know what would happen to her if she lost her voice tomorrow?" he asked belligerently.

I told him I didn't know.

"They wouldn't even come to her fucking funeral! They do it every day! I knew a woman who had a hit record. Talk of Hollywood, the whole works. She lived in constant dread of being abandoned by her fans, by her agents, and when she died *nobody* came to her funeral. Because by that time, she was a has-been, and that's a no-no in this town."

"Well," I said, not wanting to go on any longer with the course this conversation was taking, "Ritual certainly got some pipes on her."

He laid a hand on my shoulder. "Can you keep a secret?"

"Oh, yeah."

"I don't know," he said, "but I think, I don't know for sure, but I think she has a health problem. She shouldn't be giving that much of herself to her fans. I don't think her health is what it should be, but that's just something I picked up without her telling me. Just my instinct."

The door opened and Moose and Gussie came in.

"We have a lot of work to do," Moose said. "We've set up a meeting to boycott Democracy's film *Middle Passage*. The strike committee have decided to close down the set and demand that a new script be used to replace *Middle Passage*. We are going to need a script. What do you have?"

Randell took down the six scripts. "This one is about Peter Jackson," he said to us.

"What's it about?" Moose asked. "We need something very universal."

"Yeah, something they can't turn down," Tillsdale said. "What's it about?"

Winking at me, Randell said, "See, I'll show you why I wrote six." He took the scripts from the shelf. "Peter Jackson was the most graceful prizefighter to enter the ring. He fought bare-knuckled," Randell said, holding the first script. "And was dead by 1901. None of the white boys could knock him out. An Irishman named Slavin tried, claiming that no nigger would ever beat him. Prince of Wales was in the audience. Peter Jackson hit him so hard that he knocked him out on his feet! That's where the climax of my script takes place. The Irish audience thinks Slavin is just standing there taking blows. Then we cut to the audience going crazy. They think he has won! We cut to them calling Peter nigger and wanting to lynch him. Then we cut back to Slavin. He falls like a frozen corpse—he's been knocked out on his feet!" Randell slammed *Black Prince Peter* down on the desk.

"No," Tillsdale said. "With *Rocky* I, II, and III, nobody'll believe a black man existed like that. What about that one?"

"This?" Randell asked, holding the second script. "This is about Alexander Dumas père, the author of *The Three Musketeers, The Count of Monte Cristo,* and 750 other novels."

"Just a minute," Moose said. "We gotta have a script based on facts. Nobody's going to believe a black man wrote 750 books."

"No, he wrote about 1,200, only about 750 were novels," Randell informed him with a smile. "He was the highest-paid writer of his times. He got about fifty cents every time he wrote a letter of the alphabet; when he tied up his shoe, it cost him a hundred dollars."

"Yeah, but he's French black," Tillsdale objected. "We need somebody who is an American black."

"Well, I might as well skip these two, which are on the famous black duelist, Jean-Louis."

"A black sword fighter?" Moose asked, glancing at Mr. Tillsdale curiously. "Why not? People would be fascinated to know that such a guy existed."

"Maybe," Tillsdale muttered. "But let's hear about the other two."

"This one," Randell said, holding it up, "is about a black saint, Benedict the Moor. Dead in 1589, he made himself famous by his self-denial."

"Too far back," Tillsdale objected. "And that one?"

"This one is my greatest work," Randell blabbed. "The revolt of Gabriel Prosser! The first black man to lead an organized revolt against his slave masters in 1800."

"That's the one!" Mr. Tillsdale said. "Costume drama with a new twist!"

"Yeah? What's the twist?" Moose asked.

Mr. Tillsdale shook his head jubilantly. He said, *"Roots* gave everybody an indication of what white Americans want to see. Now, this will be different from *Roots* in just one way —the slaves are not happy. They are revolting."

"Do you want to read it," Randell said, handing it to him.

"I don't have to read it," Mr. Tillsdale said. "I *know* what they're looking for. But we now have another problem. We have to have somebody 'suggest' this script to them just at the moment we have closed down *Middle Passage."*

"I could do that," I volunteered. "I work in the mailroom. I do all the deliveries to the Minority Film Fund. I could just drop it on their desk."

Mr. Tillsdale looked at me with glowing respect. "You are the mailboy at Democracy?" he asked, showing surprise. "This is a *perfect* conspiracy, then." He smiled. "When the servants conspire against their masters. You take this script.

Now, when the picket line hits tomorrow you take this straight to the Minority Film Fund."

"And watch them eat it up." Moose laughed.

Mr. Tillsdale rose.

"I've got to be going," he said. "You should all get some rest. We have done good work tonight. It's morning."

I had to get to the studio.

"Good morning, fellows," I said as I went out the door.

# 16

THE next morning Tull and I stopped to buy a paper on our way to work. I was waiting in the car when Tull came back from the little corner store where we always stopped each morning to buy the paper and a coffee. "Look at that!" he said, showing me the entertainment section of the *Los Angeles Times*. I read the headline: "Blacks Angry Over *Middle Passage*."

"That's about last night," I said excitedly.

"I guess they have the full story on Moose and Randell and everybody else," Tull said as he read over the article. "Listen to this: 'Protests Erupt Over *Middle Passage:* An unfinished NBC drama about nineteenth-century Georgia plantations is being blasted by an ad hoc coalition organization for offering viewers Stepin Fetchit and Aunt Jemima clones.' "

"Hot dang!" Tull burst out.

"Man, you happy? What if they shut down the studio?"

"I wouldn't give a goddamn. I wanna go on unemployment, anyway."

"Yeah, Democracy gets away with the worst stereotypes in history. I hate to say it, but I wish somebody'd really expose them. And Uncle Gadge too. At least they could turn out some funny bullshit, but they take those slave dramas so serious!"

"Man, I was bored when the first one came out. Hey, Jonah, you know what?"

"Naw, what?"

"White man told a nigger in the South that they were going to hang him?"

"Yeah . . . ?"

"Said, 'Nigger, if we let you go, you gonna be out of town on the next train?' "

"Yeah . . . ?"

"Nigger say, 'White man, you let me go and I'll catch the train that just *left* . . . !' "

"Hahahahaha—Tull—you crazy!"

We drove on.

"Listen, Tull," I told him, "I almost had them last night. I could feel it, man. But something was missing."

"What? I thought you were funny. What was missing?"

"I don't know—I want my own style. Why can't I get it?"

"Maybe you should just let go? You know, be really spontaneous?"

"Yeah, but *how?*" I asked him, just as I turned the car into the studio turnstile entrance. Then I saw it and I think Tull saw it just when I did. There were five or six people, black and white, standing in a line just in front of the studio, carrying placards on sticks.

"Hey, man, ain't that the picket line?" I asked Tull.

He leaned forward to see better. "Hey, that's right!" he said excitedly. "That's the picket line!"

I drove the car up to the gate and one of the black women in the line looked very familiar to me.

"Join us!" she shouted to me. I recognized who she was by the voice. She was the sister in the red jumpsuit at the Black Media Forum who had the two teenagers.

"Hey, I'm with you," I said to her. "I like what you're doing."

She smiled back. "Y'all know somebody's got to do somethin' don't you?" she said to me. I was close enough to reach out and shake her hand.

A picket tried to push some pamphlet in the window.

"Listen, we work here," Tull said.

"Yeah, that's the problem," one of the picketers yelled back. "Don't work there! Join us to close the sucker down!"

"We have to get in," Tull shouted back. "We're with you!"

"Okay, tell everybody else inside," one of the others said, and they moved aside and let us through.

"Can you believe that?" I asked him as we drove through the gate.

"Well, man, what you expect?" Tull said, with a great air of nonchalance. "This *is* Hollywood, isn't it?"

We came around the corner and ran into a group of extras —cavalry on splashing horses surrounded the car so tightly we could hardly move. They were from a picture about the Civil War; the banners furling were scarlet, blue, and snowy white.

"I wish they'd move," Tull said. "Who's the A.D.? You know these guys shouldn't have the streets blocked like this!"

"You're right," said an extra who had overheard Tull. "They shouldn't have us standing here blocking the traffic, but we have to stay here until the assistant director tells us what to do."

The morning sun felt warm on my arm. I had begun beholding the brown faces of some of the actors. Each was a picture, each negligently waiting for the action to start. The props made me think I was in a surrealistic world.

Finally, the assistant director showed up and moved the cavalry on. There were piles of horse shit all over the ground when they rode away.

"I'll find out what the old man is saying about the strike," I told Tull as I turned off the engine. "And I'll tell you everything at lunch."

"Let me take *you* to lunch, then," he said, getting out of the car. "I'll take you to the commissary."

"I don't give a shit," I said. The commissary was where all

the big-time producers wined and dined their prey. "Where d'you want me to meet you?"

We were walking away from the car. "At the Kiosk," Tull said.

"Check," I said and hurried to the mailroom.

"Good morning, sir," I greeted Mr. Reese. Evilly, he glanced up at the clock. "Aren't you late?"

"Five minutes? Yeah, if you wanna look at it that way," I said. "But I was held up by the strike."

I watched his reactions out of the corner of my eye.

"Strike," he said. Then, pretending that it was an afterthought: "Oh, those lunatics." I sat down and read the first few pages of *Black Thunder*, all the while pretending that I was sorting my mail. It was a brilliantly written, true story of a tragic figure. A sizzler that unfolded like a detective novel, it had an unexpected reversal at the end.

I picked up my mail, and made my first stop at the Film Fund for Minorities. I dropped the mail off to Fran and picked up what she had, but just as I was about to go out the door, Clea came out from her office, and seeing me, but talking to Fran, she said, "Do you know what they're demanding? A slave-revolt story."

Fran looked up and saw me and said, "What do you think of that?"

"Were you at the Media Forum last night?" I asked Clea.

"Yes, I was. I thought it was incredible," she said.

"All the speeches were good," Fran said.

"Do you have a minute," Clea said. "There's something I want to ask you."

I went into her office, and closed the door.

"What does the strike committee want?" she asked me, seating herself behind her desk and beckoning me with a wave of her hand to the sofa next to her desk.

"They have a script they want to replace *Middle Passage*."

154 |

"Jonah, we are going out of our fucking minds!" Clea exclaimed. "What are we gonna do? I'll lose my job. Can you help?"

I sat my mail pouch down and took out the *Black Thunder* script Randell had given me.

"This is the screenplay the strike committee wants to do," I told her, and laid it on her desk.

"What! You have the script they want to do? My God, that's worth its weight in gold!"

Snatching up the script, she flipped through the pages as if she expected something to jump out of them. "The title is excellent," she gasped. "My God ... Jonah, you've saved me ... you've ... What a brilliant idea!" she said, glancing up at me again. "Jonah, it's a terrific story."

"But you haven't read it," I told her.

"I know, but I can tell it's just what we have been looking for," she said. "Now, let's see . . ."

"Do you think I should show it to Mr. Grayeye III?" I asked her, just to see her reaction.

"Yes! . . . No! . . . Yes! . . . Wait! . . . I got it," she spurted incoherently. "Here's how it's done. You take the script to him. You tell him it's a script that you like. If he likes it, you tell him that you got it from me. If he doesn't like it, you *don't* tell him you got it from me. That way, I'm covered."

"What do you mean, you're 'covered'?"

"That means if he doesn't like it," she said, lighting up another Virginia Slim, "my taste and judgment won't be out of line with his. If he does love it, I'll be the one who sent it to him. I'll be in line to be the producer."

"What about me? Why should I do this for you?" I asked her.

"Jonah, you gotta help me," she pleaded. "My ass is on the line this time. This picketing and protest against *Middle Passage* is directed directly against me. I chose that film for production because I thought it would help black people. Nobody told me blacks were going to be offended. Now I think somebody owes me one—a favor, I mean."

"Well, what do I get out of it? Now be specific," I said.

"If Mortimer Grayeye III loves this, I'll get you twenty-five thousand dollars and an associate-production title," she promised.

"And what about the members on the strike committee?"

"They will be given creative roles in the film," she said. "Aren't most of them actors anyway?"

The humor of that reply didn't escape me, but I was satisfied with the bargain I'd driven with her.

"You have a deal, okay? Shake on it," I said. She shook on it and I headed for Grayeye's office.

I found Mr. Grayeye in his office at the top of the White Tower. Mr. Suckoff, Mr. Klingentight, and my Uncle Gadge were present. "Gentlemen," Mr. Grayeye said, "you have given me a piece of bunk! As I've said a million times, I'm in this business to make money! *Huge piles of money!* I don't want good reviews—I want huge piles of money! Do you klutzes understand me? I *like* bad reviews. They mean huge sums of money! I need huge sums of money because I have a huge appetite! I'm a tyrant, fer Chrissake! Now, this last film *Middle Passage* is too bourgeois, Gadge. I'm surprised at you. I thought you had more street in you than that. There're too many stereotypes in it."

"But, suh, dat's jus' whut dese here people is complaining about," Uncle Gadge said, "Said hit had too many stereotypes." I wasn't surprised to hear my uncle speak in dialect to him, too.

"Sir," Mr. Suckoff said, rising, "we either have to totally demoralize the public or either give them good movies. There is no in-between. To think that we can both rob the public and give them a good movie is to think virtue can exist in hell. I suggest we *totally* enslave the public, using all the

156 |

means at our disposal, and put in *all* the stereotypes we can get!"

"Yes," Mr. Klingentight said. "This whole doctrine that the public has a free will is totally destructive to our system. I am responding to the women's demand for better films by giving them *more* racist and sexist stereotypes."

"Okay, now what do you think, Gadge? I have reports that the blacks on the plantation are acting strange. Their behavior has changed. Any servant who stands over our shoulders as they serve our food is acting strange. Is there a conspiracy going on?"

"Nah, suh," Uncle Gadge groveled. "Non dat I knows of, suh!"

Gee Wiz. Gee-Gholly. Could it be that this was the same Uncle Gadge who so eloquently defended his bourgeois films to the Media Forum?

"Well, why are there picket lines out front?" Mr. Grayeye demanded of him. "Why are the women saying *Middle Passage* abuses them?"

Uncle Gadge shifted uneasily. I could tell what was going through his mind. He was thinking how he was going to support his whores and cocaine habit and buy Aunt Lottie a new Seville if the strike killed his film.

"Well, suh," he said, "I think dat dis whole protest is just overblown."

"Overblown, my eye," Grayeye thundered. "If the networks don't pick up my film, I'm out of *four million bucks!* Gadge, don't I pay you enough money to come up with a good idea to exploit your people?"

"Yes suh, you does."

"Well, why are we having these problems?" he asked, shaking a copy of *The New Yorker* in his hand. "Last night I read a good review of my last film! How many times have I told you writers, I don't *want* good reviews. I want *bad* reviews!"

This is a good time, I thought, to give him the script. "Sir," I began, "there is a script from the Minority Film Fund." I handed him *Black Thunder*. He took it and was about to throw it aside on the desk.

"Sir, Clea Menchan read it and thought it was a good film to replace *Middle Passage* with."

"Listen, Jonah boy, Clea Menchan is a hired employee here," he said, flipping through the script. "What a nice title —*Black Thunder*. Say, I like that. What does it mean?"

"Just before the revolt, the clear skies of Virginia are suddenly filled with black clouds. A great rainfall overshadows the whole area. It's a symbol, sir."

"Did you write this, Jonah?"

"No sir."

"I like it! I like symbols. Symbols are great. Though, to be honest with you, I don't know if Aristotle recommended them in his *Poetics*. Did he, Jonah?"

"No sir, but he did mention metaphors as figures of speech," I told him.

"Isn't it amazing," Mr. Grayeye said to his aides. "I pay you shitheads hundreds of thousands of dollars a year and you give me crap to produce. And this kid here who went to a third-rate black college in the South is the one I talk to about the most important book ever written!" He shook his head and sighed deeply. "Jonah," he said, "what is this script about? A revolt? What kind of revolt?"

"Slaves revolting against their masters, sir."

"Slaves revolting against their masters? Did slaves revolt against their masters? I wasn't aware that they did. I thought all slaves were happy to be in America." He slipped Gadge an evil look, and then smiled at me.

"What a wonderful idea for a movie! It has the first important ingredient—*a simple powerful theme!* It has unity of action—that means, either they win the revolt or they do not! Second, there is conflict of major importance. Tell me, Jonah, what is the hero like?"

"Well, sir, he gave his life for his freedom."

"That's it! That's the movie I want to make. *A hero who gives his life for his freedom!*" He started flipping through the script. He saw something he liked and started reading.

Uncle Gadge, Mr. Klingentight, and Mr. Suckoff sat mute in defeat. "Listen to this," Mr. Grayeye said, reading from Randell's script. *"The slave girl Juba stripped of her clothes.* Cut to: *Slave Master Grower: As he pulls back the whip.* That's a great scene! The public loves masters-whip-the-slave-girls scenes! With a scene like that, I'll have the slave girl be beautiful and unrepenting. She grabs the whip from the slave master and begins to whip *him!* How's that for a twist?"

"But that's not in the script," I said.

"That's all right," he said, "we'll *put* it in there."

I rushed back across the lot to Clea's office. When I broke into the door, she and Fran were dancing on the ceiling.

"We're saved," she exclaimed and gave me a big juicy kiss right on the mouth. Grayeye had called her and congratulated her on getting him a script.

"I'm recommending that you be a producer," she said. "And as soon as the picture starts you'll get paid. Now, can you be at my house tonight? I want to treat you to something nice."

"What's that?"

"Dinner," she smiled, and, fool that I was, I agreed to meet her at her house in the Benedict Canyon.

But then I realized that we had more business to take care of. "Will you call Randell at this number," I told her, "and tell him his script has been bought."

"Yes, we'll make a deal with him right away."

"Goodbye. See you tonight."

Yes, yes, yes.

At lunch time I went to meet Tull. He was waiting for me right in front of the Kiosk, smoking a cigarette, a Kool. Instead of taking me to the place where the technical workers eat, Tull took me to the Celebrity Room, where all the big-shot producers and actors went. When the maître d' asked him for his name and if he had a reservation, he said, "Yes," and when she asked what name the reservation was under, he said, "Mr. Black." Now, she knew he was lying, but what could she say? You could tell that Tull wanted to impress me by taking me to this place to start with, and then to top it off, he pretended he had reservations!

Now this female maître d' was one of these really ugly white people—you know, she had this face that put you in mind of Frankenstein's fucking monster or somebody. Her skin was greenish-looking—I swear to God. She looked just like that monster in *Alien*. And her eyes were completely independent of each other.

One eye would be looking at Tull and the other one would be looking at me.

But what was so weird was when she looked down on the reservation list, there was a Mr. Black. So she had to seat us. We got these seats right beside these incredible creeps. I mean, it was a really big fucking deal. On one side was this old producer that was about two thousand years old sitting with this really yummy chick. And he was telling her all this crap about how he just knew she was perfect for this particular part in this crummy movie he was producing and she was just grinning and eating it up and trying to be cool. And while he was talking he had his hand under the table on her leg, feeling her up. Every so often she would turn and give me this shit-eating grin, and I just about threw up. Then on the other side of us were these black actresses that were playing hookers in a *Baretta* episode. Boy, were they on an ego trip. They were dressed like hookers with big brown breasts spilling all over the place, and showing nice, round, fine asses every time they moved, and, believe me, they were just moving all *over* the place. These white guys that came to sit with them almost fell over themselves trying to get next to them. The really tall one kept kissing this one white guy on the cheek and saying what a sweetheart he was. If you had seen him you would have known what kind of sweetheart he was. She was practically asking him to put cash money on the table. And Tull didn't help matters any. He kept complaining loudly for everybody's benefit how hungry he was, and when the waitress brought the menu, he let on, in a real loud voice, that he wanted some soul food. But you should have seen the waitress that waited on us. Boy, what a knockout. She was this really fine sister that had skin just like a chocolate bar and really nice knockers. When I saw her, my mouth turned to water. I swear to God. She and I got on the same wavelength—*instantly*. After I placed my order I asked her for her phone number and she started smiling, and as soon as I saw that, I knew I had me some action. She actually gave me the phone number and told me her name was Jewel. But when Tull saw me getting all this play, he got jealous and started analyzing the sister, talking about how he had *seen* her before. You could tell he hadn't *seen* her before. But while we were sitting there, these producers with their black actresses got up and old sourpuss came, just leading Randell and Stan Krass to sit down right next to us. We were sitting almost on top of them. We were practically eating off the same plate we were so close. Stan Krass was one of the most notorious sharks at the whole studio. Very aggressive. He's the kind of producer that thinks he's doing you a big favor for just taking you to lunch. You ought to be thanking God for just talking to him.

"Okay, let's say I sold you the screenplay for twenty-five thousand. What's the next step?" we heard old Randell say.

"The next step is that we draw up an agreement." He took

a napkin, and took out a pen. "Look, I'll write up an agreement now. The secretary can retype it, and you sign it."

Krass wrote out the entire contract on a piece of napkin. Tull and I exchanged looks of utter disgust. It was the old napkin trick. Even we knew about that one. Randell would sign this agreement, but when the secretary typed it up many clauses would be added to give him none of the authority he believed his contract contained.

Meanwhile, back at our table, Jewel had brought me my soup.

For what I'm about to do, I bet myself, posterity will forgive me.

With the bowl of soup in my hand, I rose from the table like I was a waiter. I turned to Krass's table and I deliberately fell forward, discreetly aiming the bowl for Krass's lap.

"Excuse me!" I shouted loudly, even before the sluppy soup had reached its goal.

"Yiieeehhhh!" screamed old Krass as the soup slurpped over his lap.

"I'm sorry, sir," I apologized, as the waitresses rushed to Krass, giving me the opportunity to tell Randell not to sign that napkin. He got it, he was no dummy. Then I rushed back to our table. But by this time this white boy came up to the table and said we were sitting at somebody else's table. Tull didn't let on like he had made a mistake, but tried to grandstand the guy, saying in a real loud voice that his name was Black, and he had made a reservation under the name of Black, and so on. Then all these white people were looking over at our table, and Tull was talking all this trash. I mean, nobody in this world can spread like old Tull. After he finished with these whiteys they went away, and old Tull, you could just tell he was feeling good, started eating his salad like he was a prince or somebody. Then in came this white boy again. This time he had a black man with him and a policeman. The black man did the talking this time. He repeated what the white boy had said. Now everybody was really looking at our table. I looked up and saw Jewel with my hamburger and she looked so good that I knew that I wasn't about to get up and leave without eating that hamburger she had put down in front of me. Then the next thing I knew I had stood up and said something to the brother in a real low voice, and he smiled and apologized and turned and knocked into the white boy standing behind him, and they left, taking the policeman with them. Tull said I told them off, but whatever I said was inspired by the presence of Jewel. In the end, everything turned out all right, but I never wanted to repeat the experience again. But almost every time I do something with Tull it turns out strange.

# 17

WHEN he was walking me back across the lot, Tull turned to me. "You know this studio is full of gooks and geeks, don'tcha by now?"

"No, what do you mean?"

"These girls who work here—they'll do anything."

"Like what?"

"Oh, man, you'll find out," he laughed.

That afternoon I had to deliver the mail I sorted out before lunch and I did find out what Tull had vaguely hinted at.

I knocked on this door, and a secretary answered it. She was new but she was young and very good-looking just like they all are. Uncle Gadge—it was his office—always gets these really fine ones, boy.

"I got something for Gadge," I said. "He in?"

"Whatja got? Oh, is that from Krass?"

"Yup."

"Gimme it here." She was a redhead, with glasses.

"I'm suppose to deliver it to him personally."

"Is it changes?"

"Probably notes to make on the changes, I think. Where is he?"

"Over in sound stage 25. Wanna take it over to him—or leave it here?"

"I can run it over to the sound stage."

"Lemme call first and see if he's still there. What time is it?" She glanced up at the clock. It was something to two. Twenty-five to two. She got the number. "Hey, is Gadge there? He is? Good. There's a package for him. A letter," she corrected, looking at it in my hand. "Send it over? Okay." She hung up the phone. "Why don'tcha take it right over to him, okay?" She was chewing gum. She smiled at me. "I got something fer ya," she said, and handed me their mail. Oh, what a great one she was. What I did was I dropped it in my bag. She looked down and saw my semi-hard-on. She went bonkers. She really did. Man, that bitch's eyes popped wide as the moon. "C'mere a sec—hey," she said. She'd stopped chewing the gum. She took the chewing gum and placed it on the tip of her tongue. She had this tongue, man, that kept crawling out of her mouth for about an *hour*.

"C'mere for a sec!" she repeated. I went over to her. She was sitting down in this chair behind the desk. I went over there and stood behind the desk like an idiot. She grabbed my ass in both her hands and hugged me to her *face*, not unlike my groin was a pillow. She closed her eyes and started rubbing her face across my hard-on like a cat washing his face or something without even unzipping me or anything. That just about ran me crazy. She kept doing this like a madman. I could feel the heat of her tongue. It was hot as hell and she kept making these sexy sounds.

"OOOOOOHHHHH! AH, AHHHHHHHHH! UHHHHHHHHHH!"

And then she whipped down the zipper and took Johnson out and looked at him.

"Oh, you beautiful black *prince!*" she exclaimed. "Oh, you young, black prince!" Having said that, she started gobbling it down like a madman. "OH, YOU BEAUTIFUL BLACK PRINCE!" GOBBLE-GOBBLE. "OH, YOU BLACK PRINCE, YOU BELONG IN THE HALL OF FAME!" Belong in the Hall of Fame!—now, that was the best I'd ever heard. Next thing I knew, I was about to come. She felt it and kept patting me on the ass. "OH, COME BABY! COME BABY! YOU BLACK PRINCE!" She'd stopped calling Johnson a prince and started calling me the prince.

"OH, MY LAWD! WHAT'S GOIN' ON IN HERE!"

Boy, I looked up and there was Mr. Reese standing in the open door! MR. REESE!

"JESUS CHRIST!" he exclaimed. "YOU PERVERTED MOTHER FUCKER!"

Boy, you'd have thought he was a policeman. Man, he came after me. I managed to get around him and make it to the door. Whew!—what a narrow escape that was. I felt like Perseus getting away from Medusa.

Going over to the sound stage, I wondered about the red-head. I wondered if Uncle Gadge had her in the office there giving it to her after he got her high on cocaine. It really killed me how dumb these secretaries were. All you had to have is a little cocaine and you could have any woman in Hollywood. I'm not kidding, I swear. If you saw a really attractive girl and you had some cocaine all you had to do is go up to her and slip it to her and tell her to go to the bathroom and take a snort. Once she does that, you have her and can do with her anything you want. I swear. Anybody who knows anything at all about Hollywood knows that. I'm not whistling Dixie, either.

When I got to the sound stage, the red light was on, so I had to wait to go in. I sort of cracked the door, though, to see what was going on in there. They were doing one of the scenes from *Middle Passage*. As you already know, *Middle Passage* was supposed to be about how black slaves came to America. The particular scene they were shooting concerned mutiny aboard the slave ship. I read the script and every-thing. It's supposed to be as authentic as hell, except it ain't. The reason I say this is because I read about it. When they make movies about slaves and slave ships, they have to take out all the really authentic stuff. If the studio wants to make a movie out of a particular book on slavery, and if the book is historically accurate about slave rebellions, they have the writer drop out all of that stuff. The reason I know this is that's what Uncle Gadge does. When he first came to Hollywood he'd complain like hell if they told him to drop something out, but after they started paying him a lot of money, he stopped complaining. When they told him to drop something out, he'd just drop it out. A lot of times, they don't even have to tell him. He just drops it out on his own.

Anyway, the scene on the sound stage was about this *attempted* rebellion. To show you how the public is fooled, they had this mock-up of a slave ship on a platform that could rock back and forth. This was to give the sense of a ship rocking at sea. Behind the mock-up they had this blue-painted canvas so that later they could project live footage of an actual storm so that the audience would think this really was shot on a real sea. All this is the process called back projection. As I was peeping at all of this through the cracked door, it sort of made me think about how people are easily fooled. It was sort of funny. Here was this stage mock-up mechanically moving up and down. To get waves, they had guys with buckets of water that they threw on the mock-up where the actors were. The actors were supposed to be slaves but you could see they were just black guys from L.A. It was sort of ridiculous. Here were these grown men faking like they were slaves while some other grown men threw buckets of water on them as they pretended they were on a ship on the sea. After the camera filmed those takes, the technicians would rear-project some takes from a real ocean and then they'd cut all these takes together and show that on television and all these fools all across America will think they are watching a real ship at sea. If you tried to tell him, like I tried to tell these ignorant niggers I know in the ghetto, that these shots are really made on the lot and not on the sea and how phoney they were, you'd be risking your life. I'm not kidding. I once got in this incredible fight with these stupid niggers over *Black Sunday* when I tried to explain how they shot those scenes with the guy standing up on that blimp in *Black Sunday*. One guy was so ignorant about movies that he kept saying how they really did shoot that scene with a guy on the actual blimp. He was so mad he wanted to kill me. I could tell he would've made a terrific slave.

I picked out Uncle Gadge among the crew. He was standing there talking to this white guy. He wasn't *actually* talking, because the red light was on, but you could tell he had *been* talking to the white guy. They were watching the guys throw the buckets of water on the slaves on the ship.

Anyway, peeping through that cracked door watching those grown men throw water on those other grown men just showed you how ridiculous people are. You'd think people would realize that the reason they make all these movies about slavery for television is for the same reason they had slavery in the first place. You'd think they'd have a sense of humor about the thing, but if you think that, you're crazy, because they don't.

Next year Uncle Gadge'll be back in Oakland at the next annual Black Film Festival Hall of Fame, snowing all those high-tone coons with the same crap. Except this time he will really be able to cook because he'll be able to tell them how difficult it was to make this movie *Middle Passage.* How hard it was to shoot that scene on the open sea. One thing about Uncle Gadge, though, all the time he is being phoney up there on the podium he never lets on that it's all a put-on. He's too good for that.

The red light went off and the guy opened the door and I went in. The actors were out of the scene for a coffee break so there were all these people all over the place.

I pushed myself through the crowd and got up to Uncle Gadge. "Gadge, I got something for ya," I said.

He turned and saw me. "Yeah, Jonah, what's up? Didya watch the shoot?"

"Oh—just a little bit from the door."

"Ya like it? It's goddamn terrific!" He always was one for blowing his own horn.

"Yeah, I liked it," I told him and handed him the envelope.

"Gadge, you know there's something I never could tell you," I said, "but I think you should see to it that Lindsey has a tombstone on his grave."

"What?" He looked at me with such a bourgeois surprise. "This is no time to talk about something like that."

"You wrote a play about his death, the least you could do was see to it that he got a headstone on his grave, don't you think? It's always time to talk about people you love," I said.

He took the brown envelope I handed him and unwound the string as if Lindsey didn't matter any more. Perhaps I was naïve but I think I got to him.

"Where did you move to?" he asked, giving me a vicious look. "Do we have your address?"

"West Hollywood, and thanks for helping me," I said, and meant it.

"We just wanted to be of help to you," he said, and then he added: "Lindsey was my brother. You let me worry about him. You just take care of yourself. You hear?"

"QUIET ON THE SET!"

Mr. Grayeye stood in the middle of the set with a megaphone. "As you all know," he said in an announcing voice, "we've had a few problems with the critics of *Middle Passage*. We are striking the sets. *Middle Passage* will not be completed. We are now preparing the sets for a new film called *Black Thunder*. Those sets will be ready next week. Everybody will take the weekend off and return to work on Monday."

"Jesus Christ!" Gadge muttered.

"Okay, Gadge, I'll see you later," I said, and went across the lot to the mailroom.

I spent the rest of the afternoon in a desultory haze. All I could think about was Randell and that strike committee. I wondered how much money would he get? Would he spend his money on beautiful clothes to take Ritual out? Or would he give his money to Gussie to pay the rent? As soon as I punched the clock, Tull and I dashed home to find out.

We burst into Fountain Lanai like gang busters. Three girls were lying by the pool in their bikinis. Steve's rock music was blaring across the patio from one side. Esmeralda was stripped down to a bikini and she was sitting on the diving board reading a pornographic magazine called the *Sun*. The lesbians were lying with their heads on each other's shoulder. Gussie had the door of his apartment cracked and as soon as he saw me he yelled, and I went over.

"You heard about Randell," he said, grinning. "He sold that script, you know?"

"No lie," I asked. "Where's he?"

"Over at Dan Tanner's. We're supposed to meet them over there. I'm just waiting for you and Tull."

Tull came in a few minutes and we jumped into Gussie's BMW and headed for Dan Tanner's.

# 18

D AN Tanner's is an Italian restaurant down the street from the famous Troubadour Café. From the outside you can't tell anything about it. Once inside, though, you see the wine flasks with straw holders hanging from the ceiling, the red leather lounge sofas, the dark-lit shadows thrown by the hidden lamps, the beautiful faces of the most beautiful babes and models, the grim, serious grimaces of the rich producers.

Soon as we busted in the door, though, we saw Randell and Moose and members of the strike committee seated at a large corner table.

The maitre d' led us to their table, passing tables of awful-looking people who stared at us.

The pretty girls seated at the tables with those rich men resembled old Hollywood movie stars. One was a dead ringer for silent film star Nita Naldi. Another one was Theda Bara. Yet another one was Valeska Suratt. In perfect imitation of these stars, they walked around like vampires. One was dressed like the star of *The Serpent of the Nile,* so that her hips reminded one of the serpentine movements of Cleopatra. Another one looked so much like Lillian Gish it was as if she had been snatched directly out of *The Great Train Robbery.* Norma Talmadge, Marguerite Clark, Mary Pickford, Pola Negri, Greta Garbo, and Bette Davis—all proliferated in several reproductions. Such a mixture of cheap imitations carried a momentary fascination until you got close enough to see it for the cheap trick that it really was.

I wasn't surprised to see that Ritual Bondage—Gertrude Williams—was seated next to Randell. I took a seat right next to Denice Little, the lady with the two teenagers. I remembered her from the picket line.

"This is the first I've been involved with doing something about the media," she said. "And I'm *proud!*"

This brought on many cheers and right-ons. Wine bottles were uncorked, and orders of everything from white fish and spaghetti to lobster and clams were placed. The strike committee was picking up the check.

We retold the story of the soup and Randell laughed and said how we had saved him from a fate worse than death.

"That was as ironical as the time I went to sell a story to Norman Lear's *Good Times,*" he said. "The white producer Channing McCloud rejected my stories as not being black enough, and began to read me *his* black stories. He flat out told me that he could write better black stories than a black writer. When I asked him why, he said he'd had a black mamma back in Texas!"

We all had a big laugh off that.

"What reasons did he give for rejecting your stories?" Mr. Tillsdale asked. "I thought you sold a story to *Good Times.*"

"I did," Randell went on. "But how I was able to do it is true irony. In that same meeting Channing became very frank. 'We are looking for stories that show blacks as unemployed,' and I quote him. 'Victims of the system.' I asked him why. He said, 'Look at the Nielsen ratings and you'll see why. When we do Negro stereotypes, our ratings go up. When we do stories like the ones you told me, good stories, our ratings go down. Whites don't want to see Negroes as human beings.'"

"At least he was tellin' you the truth," Gussie interposed.

"Yes, but he was without an ounce of humor about it," Randell went on. "He kept getting up and going to the bathroom and when he came back his face would be redder and his mood a little livelier. He didn't seem like the same person. I realized that what he was doing, he was getting a drink somewhere. I could see that he was an alcoholic, as many of these producers in television are. But then I excused myself and went to the bathroom to get my thoughts together. I figured if I was going to get him to buy one of my stories, I'd better come up with one he liked. While I was in the bathroom I smelled something like liquor and I was sure that he had a bottle stashed somewhere. But where? Then for some reason I just opened the top to the commode and to my surprise there was a plastic bag with a bottle of vodka in it. I took the top off the bottle, sniffed it, and it almost took my nose off. I went back into his office and suggested we do a story for *Good Times* about the character Keith, who is a football player, who has to be home because he has a leg injury. This, I pointed out, would satisfy his requirement that the hero be both college educated *and* unemployed. He loved the idea. And I went on to suggest that because he has a leg injury and cannot play, he has taken to secretly drinking behind his wife's and family's backs.

" 'What?' Channing bellowed. 'An alcoholic?' "

" *'Right!* He hides his liquor from his wife. When he can't get a drink he's evil and cranky. His wife doesn't know what's going on. When he goes into the bedroom—or the bathroom—and gets a drink he's in a completely different mood. The wife, Thelma, is puzzled as to what caused this new change. The supporting characters on the show, J.J. and Michael, are both wondering the same thing. Then J.J. goes into the bathroom and discovers *where* he's hiding his bottle.'

" 'Why that's a great idea, a fabulous idea, but I have just one question about this story—'

" 'What?'

" 'Where does he hide his liquor,' he asked, looking me directly in the eye. I knew this was the moment that was going to make my career in Hollywood television writing or send me back to teaching English.

"He didn't even laugh," Randell said. "But called Yolanda into the office and had her write out a contract for the idea without saying another word."

Gussie growled a big belly laugh and slapped the table again.

Moose shook his head in disbelief. *"Ain't that a bitch!"*

"Lawd today!" Tull laughed. And Randell and I laughed too. It was pretty funny, though, when you thought about it.

Randell interrupted himself and squinted his eyes in the distance. "Wait a minute! That's him over there!" he said.

"Who?"

"Channing McCloud!"

We turned to look.

"Where?"

"That old man hanging on to the bar. Right at the end."

"That's him!"

"Yeah—that's Channing McCloud," Randell exclaimed. "Life imitates art."

"He's drunk, too! I'm going over and slap him up side his head," Moose said.

Channing McCloud was barely clinging to the bar. His head was drooped down on the bar with a drink in front of it. He looked as if he were studying the molecules in the glass. His eyes dropped like a burst egg yolk. Two huge bags hung beneath the eyes, and a big bumpy nose was stuck awkwardly and pudgily right in the middle of a face as empty as an open field. His chin was tucked away beneath a pair of thin, almost nonexistent lips.

"I'm goin' over and buy the dude a drink," Randell said.

"If you do, I'll never speak to you again!" Moose threatened.

174 |

"Are you crazy? This man helped me put six thousand dollars in my pocket. How else could I afford to feed so many of you niggers." Randell laughed.

"Let's have a toast," Ritual Bondage said, raising her champagne glass. "Here's to *Black Thunder,* and to Randell. May you never have to write another *Good Times* in this life!"

We all drank a good toast to the writer.

"And for your inspiration," Randell said, "I have something for you. To one of the most talented singers of our generation, and a lady I really admire." He took out a small box and opened it. Ritual beamed with surprise when she saw the diamond earrings. I looked at my watch: I had fifteen minutes to be at Clea's house. I said goodbye to them and headed for Benedict Canyon.

# 19

WITHIN a few minutes I was on my way up Benedict Canyon to talk to Clea Menchan. As I drove past those palaces esconced in green vines and the gigantic gates that sealed off Rolls-Royces, I was aware of why she had invited me to dinner. I felt embarrassed. It wasn't the convertible Rolls-Royce or the Mercedes in front of her house that embarrassed me, but the black maid who answered the doorbell. She was nice about it, though, invited me in with a soft hospitable voice that you'd have thought it was her own personal house. I noted the Oriental carpets, checked out the books that lined the walls, the tapestry with that knight fighting a dragon on it, heard the punk sound of Devo's music exuded from the hidden speakers, and found Clea waiting for me on a mink-covered Persian-style sofa. She kissed me girlishly, and referred to the mansion as a "barn"—"Oh, Jonah, I want to move out of this barn but I'm stuck here. Once you've been raised like this, you can't get it out of your blood. Just the idea of not having this makes me insecure. I would love to live in a small apartment in Hollywood, but my upbringing has made me an addict to luxury. I hate it."

"It's a barn," I said, "but a nice barn."

She thought that I was very funny, though.

We had a few drinks and drove to The Palms Restaurant on Santa Monica in her convertible Rolls. If I told you that I didn't get a big kick out of pulling up in that Rolls with this beautiful white woman sitting beside me I'd be lying because I did. I dug it all the way.

The maître d' showed us our table, and we proceeded to polish off a dozen escargots and a bottle of Dom Pérignon.

"You don't know how committed I am to making good films," Clea said. "I see black films as being the new beginning for American cinema. Like the French New Wave films of the fifties—you know, Godard, Truffaut, Bresson—you black filmmakers are in a position to begin with a new manifesto. You have a chance to have an honest discourse with your audience, because black filmmakers have never been a part of the studio system. You are not bogged down with the traditional studio's machine of manipulation."

"What's the machine of manipulation," I asked. She sounded like she knew what she was talking about.

"The studio is the machine of manipulation," she said. "Every single aspect of a film is manipulated to keep the audience in a predictable state of surrender. But what the neorealist filmmakers, like Rossellini and early Fellini, were able to do was use the camera as if it were a pencil, as if the filmmaker himself was an author. Astruc was a French critic who developed some of these theories, which he called cam-éra-stylo. Basically, these filmmakers all shared one thing with you blacks: they each had something to say. They wanted to make political statements."

I tried to remember all the things she was saying. I knew old Randell would really like what she was saying.

"I want to make a good film," I told her, "because I want to be somebody, you know what I mean? I want to be a good comedian, a good artist, to be known for my uniqueness," I told her. "I don't want just to be another person walking around; I want to do something people'll be proud of."

"I know exactly what you feel," Clea said sympathetically.

"As a woman I identify with you. Mortimer," she said, using Mr. Grayeye's first name as if he were sitting with us, "is anxious to kill all the bad publicity that *Middle Passage* has caused us. *Black Thunder* is a positive film, and thank God for that. We're going to follow Randell's script to the T. We've hired a black director, Kingsley Adam, to direct it. Mortimer feels that since it's a black script, only a black man can be the director. Mortimer will only direct a few scenes."

I liked what she was saying: I trusted her.

"All my films have been controversial and box office," she said. The waiter held a box of cigars for me. I chose a panatela. "I did a comedy on blacks on welfare, blacks in prison, and now this one—blacks in slavery."

"But, Clea, this is not a comedy," I explained as I lit the cigar. "You can't turn this into a comedy. This is American slavery. Nobody's going to buy that. I don't care if this is the Reagan Administration."

"I didn't mean to offend you," she said, "but people want to be entertained."

"Well, I'd better tell you right now. If you make *Black Thunder* as a comedy, Randell and his friends who were on that picket line are going to be very pissed off."

"Yes, but, Jonah, I've talked to Randell about all of this," she said. "And besides, you must learn to make democracy work for you too."

"Democracy?"

"Yes—Free Enterprise."

"Free Enterprise. I thought it was Freedom *at a Price!*"

She smiled. "You're so cute!"

Halfway through our meal, she saw somebody she knew. He was a thin older guy who just took a seat across from us. When he saw her he came over and spoke. Clea seemed so uptight about talking to him that I asked her who he was.

"My husband," she said, just like it was no big thing. I

watched as he returned to his table where he was sitting with this young, gay-looking guy.

"I didn't know you were married," I said.

Reaching out across the table, she placed her hand tenderly on mine. "We've been separated for some time now," she said sadly. "Our divorce papers are coming through any day now. It wasn't a very good marriage," she said, giving the back of my hand a series of little pats. "I'm much, much happier now." I didn't know what she meant by "now," though I did have some instinctive feelings about what she was getting at by touching the back of my hand.

"He must be dying," she said, now beginning to giggle about something.

"Why?"

"Because I've seen him with that guy. The guy he's with is a fag," she muttered. "And he's out on a date with him." She was laughing at her husband.

I looked at the guy he was with. Yeah, he was gay as anybody could be.

"And to think," she said, "he must be embarrassed to see me with you. He always accused me of wanting to sleep with black men. I guess both of us have been exposed."

Clea had dessert, and just as her husband and his boyfriend were leaving, her husband patted me on the shoulder and said, "Keep her happy, boy!" and walked out, giving Clea a sneer for a goodbye. "Just like him," she said. "A bastard right up to the last."

Back at her house, we had another drink and a little cocaine. We were lying back on a fur rug in the living room listening to Marvin Gaye.

"Can you do me a favor?" Clea suddenly asked me.

"What?"

She turned her back to me. "Help me with this zipper?"

"No, I can't do that."

"I can't reach it, Jonah," she insisted.

"All right, but that's far as I'm gonna go." I went on and did it, though. Zipped it down for her. What she did then, she stepped out of the jumpsuit and stood there before me in just her panties and bra.

That just about did me in. She had one of those bodies out of the magazines, I'm not kidding. I'd already known she was fine, but I had no idea she was that fine. Her breasts were large and full. She had a waist that was thin. Her hips were wide. And with them panties on, I just couldn't stand it.

"Miss Menchan—Clea, please don't do this to me. I don't want to mix business with pleasure. I just can't," I heard myself say.

"Oh, Jonah, I've been wanting this with you so long!" she said, coming to me.

Fool that I was, I did it. She threw her arms around my neck and began kissing me. Tongue and everything. I let my hands play on that big fleshy behind of hers and the next thing I knew I'm kissing her like mad.

I backed away from her. "I don't want to mix sex and business," I warned her and started for the door. "Not now."

"What d'ya mean, not now? In an hour? In a day? A month? When the film is finished?"

"No, I mean this ain't the place for it."

"Not the place for it? We are alone in a half-a-million-dollar house. Lost damn near in the wilderness. Alone. I'm naked . . . If this is not the place for it, where is the place?"

She had me there. She really did.

"What I mean is that I . . . eh . . ."

"You're dreaming some movie scene, darlin'. Really you are. This is not a movie. We *make* movies. We don't live them. Do you understand? I've been to Vassar, Jonah, I've been to Esalen. I've studied *est*. I've studied dance therapy in San Francisco. I've been married—and you saw the results of that. Now I'm a mature woman. I've earned my way.

180

Paid my fucking dues! I don't have to explain anything to anybody. I'm not living in your movie."

"Okay, I see your point," I said.

"Oh, I get it." And she laughed. "Come here, you sweet man." She held me in her arms.

"Wait!" she said. She was panting like crazy, too. "Listen, Jonah, I wanna make a deal with you."

"What kind of deal?"

"You said something about being sure the movie is made the way it's written?"

"Yeah?"

"I'd make that promise to you on one condition."

"Yeah—what's that?"

She turned her back to me and picked up the cigarettes off the table. She had a really great body, boy. I could see muscles in her thighs when she turned away.

She lighted the cigarette and faced me again. "Jonah, I can make that promise if you're sleeping with me." When she said it, she looked pretty silly. I started to laugh, but I knew she'd be offended, and I liked her too much to make fun of her.

"I didn't mean it the way I said it." She laughed, dragging on the cigarette. "But I work too hard to have a big social life." She sat down on the sofa and pulled her legs up in her arms. "I'm getting tired of coming home and using my Clairol vibrator. And besides, I like you very much. What do you say?"

I thought about how important it was to Randell to have the movie done the way he wrote it. He wanted integrity in the film. And I wanted to be in a good black film.

"But you promise you will really do it?" I asked her. She got up off the sofa and threw her arms around me again. And I could feel the heat of her sex against my leg, burning all the way through my pants.

She took my hand and put it on the mound between her legs. "Feel what you did to me?" she said.

I didn't have any choice. The next think I knew, I was down on the floor on top of her, sucking at her nipples, and she was just moaning like she was trying to wake up the dead.

"Oh, thank you, Jonah, oh, thank you, darling," she kept just going at it like that. Every time I'd put my hand on her stomach to pull off her panties, she'd start trembling like mad and I could feel her stomach just quivering beneath my hand. She must've had two or three orgasms before I could get her panties off.

When I finally got them off, I just pulled them over her long legs. Just the sight of her long legs wide open, and her pussy was just as wet as it could be. I took it in my hand and let the head of it right in. As I pushed, she let out a deep moan like somebody being murdered. I pushed a little farther and she cried out, "Oh, Jesus!" A little farther: "Oh, *God!*" I pushed more and she must've come again because she started throwing her head from side to side, her blond hair shaking all over the place. It felt like it was lodged up in there, and when I pulled it back out a little, she'd moan again. Every time I'd push in, she'd moan, and every time I pulled it out, she'd moan. So I started pushing it in and pulling it out at first slow and then fast and she went to town, moaning and screaming and fighting and slapping her long legs against my thighs and releasing them again, sticking them in the air straight as an arrow, then clapping them on my back fist-tight. We worked like that for a long time. I just did it to her and did it to her until I couldn't do it to her no longer and then I pushed her legs with my hands down against her breasts and stood up on my knees and just went to town. I meant business then. I just banged away at her sex that was standing out like a natural man. Just standing out there for me. I hit it real good and came myself.

When I woke up, I realized that we must've passed out.

"I needed that," she said, opening her eyes.

"I needed it too," I told her. I wasn't lying. I didn't know I needed it until then. I didn't really know what it was I was needing, to tell you the truth. Now I knew. I felt it was all right for me to need it too. I didn't even think about Jewel any more, I didn't even think *not* to think about her, either.

We got up and went into her bedroom. You can imagine how laid out it was. Had everything you could want in a bedroom. Fur on the bed, silk and linen almost everywhere you turned. Big windows opening onto a garden. Large bathroom with one of those sunken baths. Had a mirror on the wall. One of them big ones, too.

Of course, soon as we got in the bedroom, we were at it again. I'd look up in the ceiling mirror and see us doing it. You can imagine what it looked like—looked like a nigger in heaven, that's what it looked like. Anyway, I guess we stayed up most of the night. I'm here to tell you it was like two children—or maybe not like two children, because children wouldn't be doing something like this, or would they? What it looked like was two people who'd discovered something that neither of them knew was there between them, but once they'd discovered it, they were just as happy as they could be.

The next thing I knew, the sunlight was in my eyes. I opened my eyes good and looked over at her and she was already looking up at me. We laughed and she pulled the cover back and looked at it. Just looked at it and started messing with it, holding it and stuff, and then kissing it. I let her do it. It felt good. You ain't gonna get me to lie and say it didn't. It did. When she had it hard the way she wanted it she straddled it and put it in her and we did it that way until she came. Then I'd not had my fun, so I got on my knees from behind her and went in from underneath.

"Oh God, oh Jesus!" she went on, tearing into the sheet with her long fingernails.

"I'm coming again!" she let out and she did, but I came right with her. Then we just fell on down and went to sleep again.

# 20

WHEN I came home that afternoon from Clea's house, Gussie and Moose were sitting around the swimming pool with some beer. There were a few girls lying out in the blazingly hot sun.

"Guess you know what happened to Randell?" Gussie grinned and looked over at Moose.

I sat down and picked up one of the beers from the cooler. "No, what?"

Moose shook his head and moaned. "I can't believe it."

Gussie pointed to Randell's apartment. The door was open and a little black woman was coming out with a bundle of clothes.

"What happened?"

"He's moving out." Gussie laughed. "She's moving him out."

"Who's moving him out?" I asked.

"Ritual Bondage." Gussie laughed. "That little black woman is her maid. She sent her over to move all of his shit over to there!" And he pointed up at the white building that loomed high over us.

"He's moving into the Sunset Tower with Gertrude Williams?" I asked.

"And leaving me here in this shithole," Moose fumed. "I'm the one that told that fool to leave Berkeley and come down here. We suppose to be working together, but the first time we get some money, he ups and spend it on that broad. He turned out to be a greedy money-grabbing petit-bourgeois motherfucker!"

We watched the little maid with her red bandanna struggling with Randell's typewriter.

"You heard what he said last night," Moose went on, "about how he sold that story to *Good Times* about that alcoholic, didn't you? Well, he's the kind of brother who'd write something like that, about an alcoholic, but I couldn't do anything like that."

The maid disappeared and reappeared a few minutes later with a box of books. Just then, one of the girls turned over and gave the sun a chance to tan her other side.

"He'll be back," Gussie said, in a consoling voice to Moose. "She'll kick him out."

"I can't believe Randell would turn out to be that kind of dude," Moose bewailed his predicament. "And what happens if I don't get that part of the revolutionary slave in *Black Thunder?* What am I gonna do if he runs off with all the money?"

"You'll get the part," I promised him. I was right with Clea on who was going to be in the movie. She was on our side, but Moose didn't know it.

"When she gets tired of that nigger," Gussie said, "she'll kick his ass out and he'll be right back here. You watch."

The maid must've made her last load because she didn't come back. Gussie said, "One thing you got to say for Ritual, she sure moves fast when she wants a nigger. Just like that song, man, she's a black-widow spider. Hey, Janet!"

Janet was crossing the courtyard carrying a large purse. She must've had her hair dyed that day because it was the first time I'd seen her with hot-pink hair and heavy eyeliner.

Gussie had us laughing at her. "Look at that purse—that's not a purse, it's a shopping bag. She goes down to those department stores—Macy's, Robertson's, and Sears—and shoplifts! They won't let you in Neiman-Marcus down on

Wilshire because the store detectives recognize you!" Gussie yelled at her.

"Look at the way she looks. Why do you think anybody would walk around with hot-pink hair like that?" he said to us. Then to her he shouted: "Janet, do you know why you go around with your hair dyed pink when you know you're too old to be a punk rocker?

"Why are you wearing that hot sweater in this weather except that you're a nut who'll wear anything anytime as long as it was cheap when you bought it in a secondhand store?"

When she got to the door of her apartment she turned to Gussie and spat: "Oh? You don't like the way I'm dressed? Some people find me to be a pretty interesting dresser. I get people coming up to me in the street and saying how good I look. You don't like how I look? So what? That's only one opinion. There's as many of them as there are people. This is America the Beautiful where we have the First Amendment that gives me the right to redress your grievances and I want you to redress yourself and apologize to an elderly person old enough to be your mother!" Then she went inside and slammed the door.

We had a big laugh. "I'm going to kick her out. I'm cleaning up this place," he promised.

"As soon as I get this part," Moose said, "I'm moving."

"Not you, man," Gussie said. "Not you—others."

# The Nightly Nightmare Revisited

---

*The River, spreading, flows—and*
*spends your dream.*
*What are you, lost within this*
*tideless spell?*
*You are your father's father, and*
*the stream—*
*A liquid theme that floating*
*niggers swell.*

Hart Crane
"The River"

# 21

ONE night, about four months after I'd begun sleeping with Clea Menchan, I did a few takes on the black bourgeoisie when my uncle was in the audience. Since our film began, I had money and Tull had taken me downtown and to Hollywood Boulevard to buy some clothes, and I must say I looked like a fashion plate. I gave up my polyester togs and only dug name-brand vines. I was feeling very good and had developed more confidence on the stage.

I started off with my "White People!" routine. I took out a cigarette and struck a pose straight out of *Gentlemen's Quarterly*. Then I did a fag pose, letting the cigarette dangle from my lips, and I limped my wrist like I had sugar in it. Then I whispered to them: "White People!"

Then I started singing it to the melody of "Go Down, Moses."

I'd say I got about two laughs on that bit.

Then I took out a matchbox. "Does anybody have a cigarette?" I asked, looking directly at this blonde who was smoking. "Could I get a cigarette from you?"

"Sure," she said and extended a cigarette to the stage. I reached down and took it.

Back on the stage, I looked at the cigarette with this outrageous expression as I gasped, "My God!

"My—you've nigger-lipped it!"

What a laugh that shtick got; I'd taken them by surprise.

"Actually, I love white people." I grinned at them. Then, changing my expression to an angry militant one: "Fuck white people! White people can kiss my ass—my *rich, black* ass!"

Wheeling around, I spit at them with the venom of a full-grown racist viper. "FUCK YOU, MOTHERFUCKERS!"

"Is he serious?"

Then I grin. "Heh, heh, heh! Jest joking, boss. Didn't mean no harm. Have to get my nuts off some way, heh, heh, heh! Sorry, if'n I messed up yo' even'n, ma'am. Yes'm, I'm sorry."

I do a shuffling à la Stepin Fetchit.

The audience applauds.

Catcalls.

Then I spied Uncle Gadge in the audience and decided to ruffle his petit-bourgeois feathers a bit. Naturally I didn't think he'd take this as anything but a joke, but how wrong I was on that score I was to find out very shortly.

"Well," I said, "black people are a trip. In the privacy of their friends they all hate white people, but just try to get that out of them in front of a white person!" And the audience saw the accuracy of my aim and applauded me for it. Everybody laughed and Gadge laughed with them.

It wasn't until I was offstage that he took me by the arm and, muttering something about "having a chat with you," he took me to the parking lot behind the Comedy Club. There he unfolded a gram of cocaine and gave me a one and one. "Jonah, I just think you ought to exercise more discretion when you're up there," he started. "You have a great responsibility when you're talking to the public like that. You just don't want to give people the wrong idea."

I stood there in that parking lot and dug the old moldy-fig that was my uncle. Still sporting those polyester plaid madras sports jackets and Florsheim shoes, he was as square as they came. Me, on the other hand, I was a different story. I had on my thin green silk shirt and white linen trousers from Maxwell Blue on Santa Monica. I wasn't the dumb shit he had put up in his maid's room and I wanted him to know it. I was packing in the people and I was screwing one of the prettiest women in town, I was proud of me, and I wasn't in the mood to take any shit from him.

"Wrong idea?" I asked, as if I didn't know what he was talking about.

"Yeah, you's got to watch what you say," he said, snorting the coke off the tip of a penknife. "There are people in this town that are watching us. We *have* to be careful. I'm making a good living now and I don't want anybody getting in the way of that."

I looked at him. His balding forehead. His pudgy stomach.

"You don't want to admit that you're making money out of racism," I said wanting to needle him. I just couldn't help making him nervous.

"Now, listen," he said, "don't you forget where you come from. We are still black in a white world. There are a lot of white people out there who don't like us!"

He looked around to see if there were any white people standing close enough to hear us. He was like a thief, I swear.

I couldn't help putting him on—it was so much fun. "Uncle Gadge, you don't think racial prejudice exists in this town, do you?"

"Of course it does! Jonah, don't be naïve!" he blabbed, and I couldn't understand why he couldn't see that I was making fun of him, just as I made fun of people on the stage. Why couldn't he see that, for me, there was no difference between the stage and life. "You're naïve! Look, your own Uncle Lindsey was killed by a white man! And I don't want that happening to my children or"—he looked at me strangely— "to you. We have gone through so much! And we're not out of the woods yet! Of course these people are prejudiced, but you don't need to go around bringing it up. They don't want to be reminded of it and you can't change it—"

"Yes, but what about the truth? Isn't it my job to tell the truth, to have something to say? To get across my 'message' to them? What about your own responsibility? I noticed that you didn't write any more plays after *Black Christ?* Why? Oh, I know! Those were the *sixties* and now we are living in the *eighties?* But what about the truth of humans in *all* ages?"

He snorted more cocaine into his nostrils and wiped his nose with the back of his hand.

"Truth? Don't worry about that. This town ain't interested in truth. It's just a place to make money in. Truth is just an excuse, that's not what you have to worry about. That's what the critics write about. You're black, and this town hasn't ever been fair to us. We are not here because they want us here, Jonah. We are here because we have made sacrifices, and others before us—Paul Robeson and great people like that have made sacrifices of their lives . . . so that we may be here to make some money. These whites don't want us here making any money! It's all right to be an artist, but the moment you begin to make money—they hate you. Now that's truth!"

"I don't believe it," I said, and I didn't. "You're telling me that you're an Uncle Tom black bourgeois to make money? Well, if that's all you want to do, then good luck. I don't feel money is that important. I try to be an artist. I try to tell the truth."

"You try! That's good. We are proud of you. The write-ups you get. The work on stage. But don't say things that will reflect badly on your people! It's easy for somebody to look at what you do and see the connection between you and Stepin Fetchit and that's very bad, son. If you're going to be an artist, rise above the clowning and shuffling—"

"But I do that as a *joke,*" I protested. "Don't you see that? When I'm shuffling like that, I'm making fun of that *whole* tradition. I'm being ironical, Gadge. If you ask me to explain irony to you—"

He waved his hands as if he had to go. "White people are

194 |

ready to laugh at any black man," he said, "but be sure that they are laughing with you and not at you."

"By your standards it doesn't matter if they are laughing with you or at you, as long as they are paying you money," I said.

"Be careful that you don't embarrass your *own* people," he said. "It's not yours to give away like that or to abuse. Just remember that God gave you a talent, and if you abuse it, he's going to take it away. Now, I have told you a few things that I hope will help you. Just remember, I'm your only relative out here. Come to me if you need help and don't— *for God's sake! Don't* put our family on stage. Don't drag up Lindsey's death as you did once before. Don't make the mistake of thinking that what happens to our family is what happened to all black families. You have no right to draw that conclusion! I know it's hard to do this, but remember, one day you will be successful. Let them say he made it as a good *clean* comedian—not because he dragged his own family and race down for his own personal greed!"

"So what's the beef?" I asked him.

"The beef? Well, you've messed up out at Democracy with that *Black Thunder* thing. Now I've had to go behind you and fix it up."

"Fix up what?"

"Fix up the script."

"You mean, rewrite it?"

"I had to. I had no choice. Nobody's going to put on a slave-revolt picture like that. Now, I had to do it . . . I had to rewrite it so white people will be comfortable with it . . . I *know* what Randell was tryin' to say, but you can't say what he wants to say that way . . ."

You motherfucker, I thought, and felt my stomach drop. I realized that I had fucked up. Grayeye had gone to Gadge with our script and changed it! How could I face Randell and Moose and all those others? I had sold out, and this is what it feels like, I thought, goddamn. I saw Uncle Gadge get into his Mercedes and heard the tires grip the gravel. Leaning against somebody's car, I felt a rock growing in my stomach. It was hot: a reddish cloud of smog hung over the city as far as the Pacific. A breeze close to the ground blew gently through my linens and tickled my groin. That bastard, I thought, that motherfucking uncle of mine, that bastard.

# 22

DURING those months I saw very little of Moose and nothing of Randell. Mainly because I avoided them. I didn't want to face up to selling them out. Moose was given the role of General John in the film and earned enough money to move into the Hollywood Hills. Once Moose said he ran into Randell and told Gussie that he looked more like a Hollywood playboy than he did a scruffy writer that we had known. Occasionally, I would see him and Gertrude Williams at parties. Randell would be very well taken care of. His clothes were the best, he had new hip, blue glasses. Gertrude would always be at his side.

One evening, however, at the Le Moustache, a French restaurant, I sat not more than three tables from them. Isn't it strange that in this town friends who have struggled together begin, after making some money, to avoid each other? How was it possible that I, who admired Randell immensely, should be hiding my face behind a menu? Was it the money that made us this way?

In any case, I heard a loud argument taking place between him and Gertrude. She was accusing him of looking at an attractive blonde sitting across the room. Randell claimed he wasn't looking at her, but Gertrude got louder and louder in her insistence that he had been flirting with the blonde. She told him, "If you look at that bitch just one more time, I'm going to throw this damn champagne in your face!" Everybody within earshot waited for this little drama to unfold, and unfold it did. Having decided Randell's eye had wandered again, Gertrude flung the glass of champagne in his face and jumped up from the table and stormed out of the restaurant.

With a shitface grin, poor Randell sat there, while everybody laughed at him.

I decided this was the perfect time to assuage my guilty conscience. Like a true scoundrel, I rushed over to his table as if I had not seen what had happened, and immediately began asking him how his work was going.

"Working on anything new?" I asked him while he fished out a handkerchief from the $750 jacket—I had almost bought the same jacket.

"Yes, yes," he said, happy that I was helping him out of this slight difficulty. "I'm finishing my novel about Hollywood."

"Every screenwriter is writing a novel about Hollywood," I said. "Who doesn't have the writer's itch?"

He sort of smiled. "I guess you're right," he said. "Don't worry about Trudy. She'll be back. She gets like this. I'm use to it now."

"So what's your novel about," I said, and I saw that he was looking at my table.

"Isn't that Clea Menchan?" he asked, squinting because he didn't have his glasses on.

"Yes," I admitted. "We've been very busy making your movie."

"Well, how's it going?" he asked. "Are you shooting it just the way I wrote it?"

"We'll be very careful with this one," I told him. "We want it to be the first real black film."

"Where's Moose?"

"He moved from the Fountain Lanai. Now he's getting ready to star as Gabriel's aide—General John. Why don'tcha come to the set sometimes? Billy Badman is playing General Gabriel."

He put his glasses on then. "I would, but we're going to Berkeley," he said. "We were going together. If she doesn't come back here to apologize to me, I'm going alone. My bags are packed."

"Berkeley? You're going back to teaching?"

"No, it's . . . well, I'm not getting any writing done here. I told you I'm working on a novel, but that's not quite true. The truth is that I haven't been able to write a thing since I moved up in the Sunset Tower with Trudy. When I was living in that rat's hole at the Fountain Lanai and nearly starving to death, I was cooking. Now, I don't know what it is, but I haven't been too inspired you might say."

He laughed with a nervous irony.

"I thought Ritual Bondage would inspire at least a couple of screenplays and novels," I said.

He looked very grave and serious then. "No, she hasn't inspired me to write a novel," he said. "But she has inspired me to live one. I KNOW I've got to get away from this fucking town, man. I can't work looking down from that damn Sunset Tower. I told Trudy that, told her I had to get back to Berkeley. My bags are packed, just like I told you. I'm leaving this evening, whether she comes or not."

He seemed disturbed by something he was thinking but not saying.

"What? What's the trouble?" I asked him.

He looked around to see if Ritual Bondage had returned yet. "She'll be back," he said, almost to convince himself, and then in a faraway voice he said: "One night we went to a party given by her manager. He lived in a fabulously expensive house in Brentwood. I compared this house to the one Trudy owns in Long Beach, the one her mother and her two teenage children live in; it's barely above the poverty level. It depressed me to see how well she takes care of these guys and how her own family can barely get by."

"Why do you stay with her, then?"

"How can I abandon her?" he asked. "She needs me."

When he looked at me, he must've thought I didn't understand because he went on. "Let me tell you a story. I went to dinner at Trudy's mother's in Long Beach. She has two very nice children, as I said before. I went to the store with her son to get some wine for dinner and the liquor store was right in the ghetto. I saw the pool hall, and the hustlers, the young girls who would soon be whores, and the young brothers who would soon be in prison. I saw what I'd escaped from in Detroit. I remember one skinny black girl who worked behind the counter of the liquor store. She was humming a song as she went about getting the liquor for us, with a bunch of boys about her age teasing her about her budding breasts and hips, but she made a point of ignoring their remarks by smiling brightly and humming that tune. It was familiar and strange. This, I thought, was Trudy when she was that age, and when I left the store I carried that tune with me in my heart. After a big Thanksgiving dinner of turkey and pies, we all sat in the living room around the family album, which followed Trudy's career from the small town in Mississippi where her mother lived until one day she took up her three girls, the oldest being Trudy, who was about ten then, and headed for a new start in Long Beach, California. There were snapshots of the mother and her three daughters in Mississippi in front of a raggedy shack, with Trudy holding her baby sister in her lap, and the baby sister was almost as big as she was. There were snapshots of Trudy as a teenager, in white bobby socks, legs like skinny black bean poles. Some snapshots of her in the revolutionary sixties in a miniskirt (with the same skinny legs), and some of her when she made her first recording, and then there were the newspaper clippings tracing her rise. With her now-grown sisters and mother and children, I had a great time looking at that album, but I could not help noticing that there wasn't a man in any of these pictures. Trudy had told me that each of her sisters had a different father. She didn't know who her father was, and had never met him. Her sisters had never met their fathers either."

He stopped talking abruptly. I looked up and saw Ritual Bondage standing in the door of the restaurant. She looked magnificent, she really did. She was wearing a purple dress that clung to her shapely body for dear life. She was stacked within an inch of her life. And she was contrite.

She came to Randell's table with tears in her eyes. "Oh, darling, please forgive me," she cried, as she slipped into the seat.

He took her hand and kissed it and held her against him. "It's all right, baby," he muttered. "I'm sorry. It was my fault."

"No," she pleaded. "It was my fault, I'll try not to be so jealous! I'm working on it!"

"I know you are," he said. "Did you see Jonah was here?"

She looked up and smiled. She was truly beautiful when she smiled.

She spoke to me and went back to Randell. "Can we go to Berkeley?" she asked, as eagerly as a child.

"Okay," he said. "Okay, let's finish the champagne first."

I excused myself and went back to join Clea.

In this conversation he didn't mention anything about her health, though I was prepared to ask him since he had mentioned it to me that night when he gave me the *Black Thunder* script. I thought perhaps he was wrong about her bad health. But not more than two weeks after this encounter at Le Moustache, a strange thing happened that proved me to be wrong.

# 23

IT was a Saturday morning. Not much had changed about
the Fountain Lanai since Randell and Moose moved out.
Esmeralda was still having her daily bouts with her vibrator, and we'd become so accustomed to her open-window
exhibition that when we heard the blender-like buzz of her
vibrator we closed *our* windows. Derek was still washing
Howard's car every Saturday and taking out his garbage
each day, still hoping for a break. The Hudsons were still
taking their drives to their Malibu home in their Mercedes.
The lesbians were still fighting like cats at night, only to
be by the swimming pool the next day in each other's
arms.

Gussie was still venting his spleen on the old miserable
creature Janet. The last week had seen an intensification of
his disease and Janet was at her wit's end to escape his
relentless wrath. For the past few days he had been closing
in on her and there seemed to be nothing that would prevent
him from satisfying his irrational gratification.

The stage was set for the closing climactic scene.

I stood on the balcony listening to Derek dashing water on
that actor-teacher's car and to the humming of Esmeralda's
vibrator, and smoking another cigarette.

While I was standing there I saw Janet come into the
courtyard. As soon as the sound of her heels resounded on
the concrete, Gussie's door flew open and he yelled out,
"Janet, I want you out of this building by Wednesday!"

He was dressed in those brown safari shorts, and jingling

his keys and change with his hands in his pockets with a boastful jubilance.

She didn't stop walking.

"I heard what you been up to," Gussie yelled to her. "I'm kicking you out." Then he closed the door. I don't believe he saw me.

Janet spied me leaning across the balcony. "He hates me! He hates me!" she screamed as she rushed in.

"Who hates you?" I asked. "Who?"

"That damn Gussie!" she cried.

She strutted around the apartment like a boxer. She was a well-built woman, though her true beauty had begun its inevitable decline, as all beauty must, and her varicose veins stuck out about a half-inch from her legs, but she was still trim, and had a good figure. When she was young, she had been one of Marilyn Monroe's stand-ins.

"They said I was acting obscene," she confessed.

"Well, were you?"

"No! Hell, no! I'm a lady. Whatever I do, I do with dignity. Those motherfuckers can go straight to hell!"

"I know you're a lady, Janet," I told her. Actually she was. She really was. She was probably the only real lady in West Hollywood. But she was also evasive as hell; I wanted to pin her down.

"But were you out there in your bathing suit again?"

She looked at me as if she'd been divested of some deeply buried secret. She had begun to shake and her lower lip trembled nervously. "Who told you? They told you those filthy lies!"

"No one told me, Janet. I saw you myself."

"You saw me?"

"You're a very sad person, Janet. You'll have to admit that you're a bit strange."

"Somebody's spreading evil gossip about me and I have my suspicions who it is."

She had this bizarre notion that all her troubles with Gussie stemmed, somehow, from Celeste. Yet Janet was the only person who didn't laugh at Celeste behind her back.

"I'm going over there and put my fist in her big mouth!" she said.

"Let's go and tell Gussie he can't kick you out," I said.

"Come on," I said, taking her by the arm. We went out on the balcony and saw the Hudsons.

"Good afternoon, Mr. Hudson, Mrs. Hudson." I always respected them. They were nice people, they really were.

"Good afternoon, Jonah," Mr. Hudson said. He was wearing brown slacks and one of those white terry-cloth short-sleeve jobs, the kind with that little alligator over the pocket. He was the president of a cement company, or something like that—really a nice man.

"How's the comedic artist making it nowadays?" Mrs. Hudson asked. She had really gorgeous black hair, but it was never hanging down, always scooped up in one of those high-class hairdos you see in *Vogue*, and she was wearing a short skirt with a slit up the side, but it wasn't all the way up like the hookers and dogs like to wear, but decently up the side, and she had a white blouse, the type you can actually see through, except you couldn't see all the way through it, the way you can some blouses, and actually see a big old nipper staring you in the face, and she was wearing a pair of black, pointed heels.

"Hello, Janet," Mrs. Hudson said. They were going down the stairs then.

Janet laughed. "Ha, ha, ha!"

"Baby, you just have to be a lot cooler," I told her.

"I didn't bother nobody. I was just enjoying myself. What kind of world is this, anyway? You know what I'm talking about, now, don'tcha? What kind of world is it? Just being free!"

Mr. and Mrs. Hudson came back into view; they were in the courtyard. They were crossing over to their Mercedes parked in the garage.

I knocked on Gussie's door again. He opened it. "Come in here," he growled.

We went in.

"I run a respectable place—" Gussie started in a high, angry, bragging voice.

"BALONEY!" Old Janet shouted.

"SHUT UP, JANET!"

Janet could be a very sensitive woman. She was crying inside but she didn't drop a visible tear. All iron and steel there.

"TAKE HER OUT OF HERE BEFORE I GET MY GUN!" Gussie shouted. Janet stamped her feet like a bull stomps the ground as a prelude to his charge.

"THAT'S IT, YOU DUMB FUCK!" Janet cussed, and ran for the door. She could pitch a natural bitchin' fit when she got good and worked up and Gussie had worked her up.

Janet flew out the door and ran down the steps and crossed over to the swimming pool.

Gussie, following her out to the railing, shouted to her, "Janet—you're finished in this town! Leave!"

Then Janet did what she had always wanted to do; she stood there in the middle of the courtyard and at the top of her voice cussed out every living soul in sight.

She had her sailor cap in her hand and slapped it against her leg, holding onto that big suitcase of a purse.

"I AM A DECENT PERSON. I'M SOMEBODY NICE, BUT WHO ARE YOU CREEPS? HUH? I WANNA KNOW. SAY, I'LL TELL YOU. YOU'RE A BUNCH OF DEGENERATES!"

Everybody who was not awake was awake now. When Sultan stuck his head out the door, Janet spied him and laid him out.

"AND YOU, YOU DUMB FUCK DOPE SMUGGLER OF FOUNTAIN LANAI—HA! YOU'RE GOING TO THE SLAMMER ONE OF THESE DAYS, BUDDY, SO YOU CAN KISS MY ASS TOO!"

Sultan snatched his head back in like a turtle and slammed the door. Janet stumbled over to Esmeralda and Sharon lying on their towels and jumped back like she'd stepped on a snake.

"AND YOU—YOU AIN'T NOTHING BUT A WHORE! I KNOW YOU'LL SCREW ANYBODY JUST TO GET IN A MOVIE. SO YOU CAN KISS MY ASS!"

Then she started doing bumps and grinds like she'd been doing in front of the bus stop at La Brea and Santa Monica.

"Go get her and calm her down before I call the police," Gussie said to me.

Like cold-hearted vultures, the neighbors watched.

I went down to where she was and when I got to the railing I saw Tull coming up. He must have been up in one of those apartments screwing one of those girls that just moved in. Sneaky bastard.

As I was leading her to her apartment, I was thinking how horrible it would be if Celeste showed up at this moment. No sooner had I thought this than Celeste, dressed up and with her white boyfriend on her arm, appeared outside her apartment and stared down the steps. Hawk-eyeing her, Janet leaped out of my grasp with dog-after-cat ferocity.

"AND YOU—YOU BITCH! DO I KNOW YOUR STORY!"

Taken aback, Celeste huddled close to the white boy for protection and kept on stepping.

". . . YOU QUEEN! WHEN YOU GONNA GO BACK TO BEING A MAN?" Janet screamed at her. Celeste quickened her steps. The white boy looked at Celeste strangely.

"Oh, come on," Celeste said to him. "That woman is out of her mind."

But Janet went after her again and started talking to the white guy then.

"Say, you know she's not a real woman," she said point-blank to the guy. "SHE'S A MAN!"

"Bitch, you ain't talking to me?" Celeste said. "What you say—what? Baby, you can't read me! How dare you say those things about me!"

Alternating between flirtation and mortification, Celeste tried to fake her way out of this embarrassing situation, but Janet was heartless as a surgeon wielding a scalpel.

Janet ripped off the veil of her sexual dubiety.

"YOU HAD THE TUCK-AND-FOLD JOB! BABY, DO I HAVE YOUR NUMBER!"

Having been so flagrantly, unbearably exposed, Celeste couldn't be a girl any longer. "BITCH, I'LL KILL YOU!" She took off her shoes and threw them at Janet. "BITCH, WAIT TILL I GET MY HANDS ON YOU!" She grumbled just like a dude then, and leaped over the balcony—she was on the first floor—and landed in front of the swimming pool on her feet—like a man.

Bracing herself like a bull against Celeste's charge, Janet grabbed her blouse and tried to scratch her face; but Celeste held her with one hand at arm's length and then smacked her with a left. Jumping in between them, I pulled them apart, and caught one of Celeste's punches on my jaw for the trouble. The dude could hit, too.

While Tull held Celeste and I held Janet, they screamed insults at each other, finally breaking away from us.

This time, though, it was different. Celeste charged into Janet and Janet moved aside, allowing Celeste's momentum to carry her into the swimming pool. Janet pretended she had thrown her into the pool.

"Didn't I tell ya?" she screamed at Celeste floating in the pool. Her makeup turned the water red around her.

"Somebody get me a towel!" she pleaded. "And call the police to take her away!"

Now, all the while this was going on, the white boy stood rooted to the cement with a shocked look on his face.

Shocked, he asked soaked Celeste, "Is it true?"

Half sobbing, half angrily, Celeste screamed at him, "Get me a *towel,* you idiot! Oh, you idiot, idiot!"

Now comes the point of this story.

"There's Randell," I heard somebody say and I turned to look. He was standing in the driveway. He had a downcast look on his mug and he was carrying his suitcase. Everybody stopped and stared at him, even old Celeste. Where had he been? Why was he so depressed? What happened to his fine clothes? Where was Gertrude? Was he here to stay at the Fountain Lanai again?

Rushing Janet into her apartment, I got some brandy from the kitchen—I practically knew where everything was in the apartment—and gave it to her and shot back over to Gussie's apartment to talk to Randell.

# 24

GUSSIE met me halfway across the courtyard with a big derisive grin on his face.

"She kicked his ass out." He laughed. "Didn't I tell you she would? Didn't I? Well, she did it. Cut up his clothes, and changed the locks on the door, and then hired somebody to beat him up."

"Is he okay?"

"In there crying like a baby." Gussie grinned with satisfaction. "I want to call old Moose from your house. I don't want him to know Moose is coming over. Go on and talk to him, he's in there blubbering like a child. That bitch kicked him out."

He wasn't blubbering like a baby as Gussie had put it, but he was looking pretty badly shaken up.

With a drink in his hand, he sat on the edge of the sofa with his head resting on his knees. When I walked in, he looked up and tried to regain some of his lost self-esteem by standing up and giving me a quick smile. "Hey, Jonah," he said. "How you doing, man? How's my movie?"

"Oh, it's coming along," I said. "What happened between you and Ritual?"

"I guess Gussie told you," he laughed. "She kicked me out. I guess I can tell you now. She's had a heart attack before, and I had her go check up on her health, and it turns out she has a couple tumors in her stomach. The doctor told us if she exerts herself by going back on the stage, she has a good chance of having another heart attack. When I started bringing this up, she got mad at me and got real distant, you know. But I was more concerned about her health. She and her managers accused me of trying to stop her career. Then this happened." He gestured to his suitcase. "She just hired four dudes to come to the apartment and put me out in the street."

"But weren't you in Berkeley?" I asked, remembering our encounter in the Le Moustache. "Did you go?"

"Oh, we went to Berkeley. Berkeley was new to her and she loved it. You know, I have this little house up in the Berkeley Hills. I started writing and she explored the shops on Telegraph Avenue. She liked passing herself off as a housewife when she was shopping at Co-op—discussing the rising prices with the housewives. She even got some of them hiking boots and a backpack. Her health improved, too, and then one day a telephone call from her manager changed everything. I found out later when we were back here in Hollywood, she'd been offered almost half a million dollars to go back and perform. But she kept telling me, 'This is what I want,' this little house and me, and my writing, but she couldn't wait to get back to Hollywood. That was last week. Then she started going out to get ready for this new album this company is releasing for her, and then she started back to freebasing. Up in Berkeley she didn't even think about cocaine. Now she's just doing this stuff like it's going out of style.

"She just kept doing that freebase. Come about last week, though, she come just a-complaining about pains in her stomach. Now, I put two and two together and figure she oughta go see about them tumors. I didn't tell her this, of course, I just suggested that she go see the doctor. *See a doctor?* She got mad with me. Said she was going on a food fast to lose some more weight. She got this new album coming out so she figure she's got to look like Donna Summer.

How can she look like Donna Summer? She ain't no young chippie anymore, but if I said anything like that, she sure enough gonna get hot with me. Well, anyway, she goes on this water diet. Don't eat nothing! Now, I'm still thinking about what that doctor told her. So one morning I just up and told her, you better take yo' tail to that doctor and see about your health. I shoulda not said that! She gets hot with me and leaves the house and don't even come back until the next day! Now, another thing I got to tell you. Trudy is a fairly good-looking woman, I grant you. But she told me she hated her nose, said it was too big, and she was going to get a nose job. I figure she's just saying this. Well, I figured wrong. She's about as unhappy with her looks as a person can be. Come to find out, she hates being black. Why? Because all symbols of beauty in this town is white blond women! That's how come she always roll her eyes at me if we're in a restaurant and a white girl walks by or sits down at the next table. Yeah! Here I am thinking she's a queen and here she is hating the way she looks! On top of that, she got this bad case of stretch marks on her stomach. Stomach all folded over like the Buddha's. Didn't bother me none, except she'd say to me, 'You can't stand my stomach, can you?' Kept saying this, kept saying it. Finally she ups and just flat out tells me that the reason she gets so jealous when I go down to the pool to swim is that she's sure I'm looking at those white girls' *flat* stomachs! Boy, did she tell me a lot about herself when she confessed to that! Then, seems like after she told me this, she sorta got ashamed she told me, like she didn't trust me no mo'. And then on top of all this, she starts reading this book by Dick Gregory called *Cookin' with Mother Nature*. I saw her reading that book but I didn't pay it no mind, till one morning I turned over for some action and she come tellin' me Dick Gregory said in that book you ain't suppose to have sex when you're fasting. Imagine Dick Gregory writing a thing like that and he got eight children! I told her I didn't give a damn about Dick Gregory. He ain't no Father Divine and that I wanted some action! Now I shouldn't've said that. She jumped up in bed and told me, I'll have you killed, motherfucker. Now *she* shouldn't've said that, either!"

"She threatened *you?*" I asked. "Told you she'd have you killed?"

"I doan like nobody saying stuff to me like that. My Uncle Jack was shot and killed by his old evil black wife while he was sleeping in his bed on a Sunday morning. So when she said that, I just said to myself, 'Randell, it's hat time.' By 'hat time' I mean it's time for me to get my hat and leave. Then she don't come home until the next day. I'm up in there on the telephone talking to another writer friend when in she walks with four big football-size dudes. I say to her, 'What the fuck do they want?' She says to me, 'I want you outa here.' I said, 'Baby, you got it.' I grabbed my things—mostly books, I even had her reading books, you know—and split, but I still love her and will do anything for her.

"She pretended that everything was all right, but I knew better. She was about to get a lot of money. Now, what has happened is that these white boys had told her that I was bad for her career. They got to her with some good drugs and told her she could legally hire four thugs to kick me out. But what they didn't tell her was that I love her and they don't. I want to see that she lives a long time because I love her, whether she is rich or poor. But she cannot see this because her managers are pimping her. And I'll tell you this. If she continues to go at the pace that they want her to, she will collapse on the stage from a heart attack. Now, Jonah, you must help me."

"How?" I asked.

"You know Democracy owes me my bonus of twenty-five thousand dollars. I'd like you to help me get it."

"No problem," I told him.

"Now, I've heard that the film has been changed," he said.

"No, that's not true," I said. "The producer Clea Menchan is a friend of mine. It's not been changed."

"Did you keep them from destroying my movie?" he asked. "Because if they don't change it, it'll be a good picture. And if it's a good picture, Trudy will come back to me. Don't you see, I've got to get her back? I still love her more than anything in this world. She has to know that I'm an artist, that . . ."

"You expect her to be impressed?"

A painful look settled into his face. He was fighting something inside, but the battle was taking place in his face.

"She'll see that I am an artist," he said. "If they don't change my script, she'll see that. I want her to know that I am a writer."

"Wouldn't she just like you for yourself?" I asked him. "I mean, you know—even if you weren't a writer?"

He scowled and reached for the bottle of bourbon sitting on the table.

"You want her respect. I can understand that."

I watched him pour a drink and kill it and pour another one.

"I want her back," he said. "I love her and miss her."

"You do? Well, why did you leave? Were you mean to her?"

"I might've been," he said. "But I didn't mean it. I just wanted to show her that I am a real writer. Seems like everything went against me in the last month or so. I couldn't sell any scripts. All the producers started turning down my scripts. And Ritual began to watch this. When she saw me gettin' rejected she turned against me. But with this one," he said, shooting a sharp glance at me, "I am gonna show her! She'll see!"

Just then Gussie came back into the room.

"I've got a place for you," he said. "Not as big as the one you and Moose had before, but it's a nice one."

"Good," Randell said.

Gussie laughed.

"Man, I hate to say this, but she just sported you for a real sap! She's probably not as sick as you think. I saw her not long ago, driving a new Seville with a white boy riding so close to her that it looked like the dude was *under* her."

I guess Randell needed Gussie to tell him that! But he took it like a gentleman. He didn't even wince.

Not more than five minutes later, Moose came in. "Man, I told you that broad wasn't any good," he started. "I'm sorry to hear what happened to you, man."

"That's all right," Randell said. "Man, I heard they changed my script, did they?"

Moose had profited a great deal by Randell's script, to judge by the new style he was sporting: gold chains hanging from his open shirt, his expensive cowboy boots and matching summer suit.

"There aren't enough lines for the slaves," Moose said. "All the long speeches seem to go for the slave masters. You didn't write it like that, did you?"

"Naw, they changed my script." Randell said. He was guessing, but he was guessing correctly.

"I don't think they did," I told him, and was probably too depressed to tell him Gadge was rewriting it.

"I'll leave a pass for you to come on the set tomorrow," I told him, "and I'll go read the script and see if it has been changed."

Moose laughed. "They had been giving us our script each day," he said. "We never get the whole script. I think that we will shoot a rescue scene tomorrow down by the lake."

"Okay," Randell said.

When I walked out of Gussie's place, Esmeralda was basking in the sun by the pool. Janet was inside her apartment. Celeste had recovered, no doubt. It was as if nothing had ever happened.

Dreading that Moose was right, I left to go to the Comedy Club. I was working that night.

# 25

WHEN I walked into the Comedy Club that evening I had a big surprise waiting for me. My old friend Buddy had returned from Santa Cruz. Grabbing me just as I walked into the back of the club, he let out a big yell of pleasure. It was good to see him, too.

"It was too peaceful up there in Santa Cruz," he said, when we got a table, and a couple beers. "I got bored after about a couple of months. My poetry didn't turn out like I wanted it to. And the teaching was a joke—a real joke. All I was doing was baby-sitting these soft-behind rich kids. I don't think they were really interested in literature, anyway. Then I missed L.A. I missed the noise of the traffic, the cops beating people upside the head, the smog."

"You missed the smog?"

"Yep," he said. "I know it's hard to believe, but I missed it. I missed almost choking to death every time I took a breath."

"So what're you going to do now?"

"Get back into comedy," he said. "It's nice to have something to come back to, huh? Maybe me and you can team up after all?"

I must've been looking pretty down in the mouth that night, because Buddy noticed it right away.

"What's eating you, Young Blood?" he asked. "What happened at the studio?"

"Aw nothin'," I said. I really didn't want to talk about it.

I didn't see how you could talk about it. I knew the studios lie to writers about their work, but every time I thought of old Randell, though, I started feeling sorry for the dude. Buddy smiled quickly. "I don't believe that," he said. "I know something's gone wrong with you. Who's the girl?"

"Clea—Clea Menchan," I had to tell him. I felt like a drink real bad. "I see a lot of dirty stuff where I work, you know?" He gave me an inquisitive look. "So? What do you expect?" he said. "This *is* tinsel town."

I stopped the waitress and ordered a gin.

"I know that, but when you see it happening to somebody you know, it's different," I said.

"You mean your friend Randell Young?" he asked. "What happened?"

"He wrote this script *Black Thunder* and it's a very good script, but the studio has rewritten it as *Uncle Tom's Cabin*," I said.

"Ha, ha, ha!" Buddy laughed. He thought I meant it as a joke.

"No, I'm serious. Mr. Grayeye's been trying to do an Uncle Tom's Cabin picture for years. Uncle Tom's Cabin, you know, was very popular everywhere it was shown. It was a block-buster, a runaway success. This is what the studio is looking for. So they tried to do it with my Uncle Gadge's *Middle Passage*, but protest groups made him cancel it."

"Yes, I remember that," Buddy said.

"Now, Randell Young sold them a good revolt script, which the protest groups approve but—"

"—The studio is trying to rewrite it back to the old script," Buddy said.

"Yeah—and they are screwing Randell in the process," I explained. "The other day my uncle told me he had rewritten it. I saw them tell him they weren't going to change his script. Now I feel guilty, I don't know what to do."

"The first thing to do is tell Randell," Buddy said. "Let him know so he can protect his work. If he loses his work, he is lost in this town."

The waitress sat the drink down and I took a sip of it. A calmness settled quietly in my stomach. Tonight was just another night at the job. Yes, Buddy was right. I had to tell Randell, and get him on the set while they were shooting a scene. He would be able to tell they weren't his scenes.

"You should read the story he wrote," I said.

"What's it about?" Buddy asked.

"Gabriel Prosser's revolt," I said. "Of course the niggers get caught and hanged in the end, but it's revolutionary until then."

"Really? And they accepted it?"

"Most of it," I said. "But they changed it and had a scene where Uncle Tom has to save Little Eva."

"What? You kiddin'?"

He just didn't believe me.

# 26

I was standing on the set of *Black Thunder,* but there was the steamboat, and the actor dressed up like Uncle Tom, and the little blond girl who was to play Little Eva.

I saw Clea Menchan talking to the black director, Kingsley Adams. I went over to them, and asked to speak to Clea. "Listen, I'm embarrassed that we are shooting an Uncle Tom scene in *Black Thunder.* How do you justify such a horrible thing in Randell's script?"

She looked good enough to eat in a white straw hat and white linen dress.

"Mortimer's idea," she said. "The decision was made before I knew anything about it."

"But you could've at least told me," I said. "I'd've stopped it. Now what about Randell's bonus?"

"Krass told me that according to the contract he is not entitled to a bonus if the script is changed."

Just then I saw Randell coming onto the set. I knew he was angry when he saw the steamboat and all those actors that had nothing to do with what he had written.

"You changed my script!" Randell yelled. Clea turned and saw him. He didn't look too happy, to tell you the truth. I went over to where he was shouting at Stan Krass.

"What happened to my script?" he shouted at Krass. "You have changed my script!"

Krass was trying to calm him down. "Randell," he kept saying, "we talked about this. I told you there was a few scenes that had to be written over."

Randell was shaking his finger into the dude's face and screaming down his throat. "I didn't have any Uncle Tom scenes in my script! Who put this Uncle Tom saving Little Eva shit in here!"

"Randell," Clea was pleading, "let's talk about this in the office. This is so unprofessional!" She said, spying me: "Jonah, talk to him."

"I don't like to be a difficult person," Randell said, "but I didn't write a rescue scene in my script. How did it get in there?"

Kingsley turned to Stan. "Stan, you told him we had a rewrite on the script, didn't you?"

"Well, I talked to him," Krass conceded insincerely. You could tell he was guilty as hell. His face suddenly got lobster-red.

"Yes, we had a meeting in the commissary," Randell admitted. "But you swore to me that you'd not hire another writer. As a matter of fact, we put it in the contract."

"Oh, no, we didn't," Krass lied right through his teeth. "I'd never do a foolish thing like that." I was right there, though, when Randell had him put it in the contract.

"You're cheating me," Randell said coolly.

"Fran? Go get those contracts. See if they're not in my briefcase," Krass said, twitching his lips cruelly at Randell.

One of the assistant directors yelled down from the steamboat. "We are ready to go with Little Eva falling in the water. Are you ready down there?"

Up on the steamboat, the little girl was standing with a blanket around her.

She was on deck with the Uncle Tom actor.

"No—hold up," Kingsley instructed him. "We gotta problem."

"Yeah, we do have a problem," Moose's voice boomed out. He was coming from the other set with a bunch of other actors. Most of these black actors were naked from the waist up. A Creole *marchande des calas* came up peddling rice croquettes to the other actors. Another black actor who looked so much like the Candjo Creole-born chief that my eyes forgot to make the mind distinguish between the role and reality. About twenty-five other blacks, their bodies muscular and naked, moved up to us with Moose leading them. With an old blunderbuss flintlock thrown across his shoulders, Moose strolled up to Krass.

"I don't like this script," he said to Krass. "You fucking people tried to cheat us. You waited until the strike was dissolved and you tried to pull this shit!"

Stan looked at Moose and paled. Dressed like a slave, Moose was the real Mandingo—he wasn't playing; with his muscular body naked to the waist, his magnificent head was mobile with energy, his nostrils flared with anger, his lips thick with insolence, his eyes glistened with a shifting glint of evil.

"Now just a minute, fellow," Stan said. Behind Moose several slaves were waiting to make the shot. Several of the black actresses had their breasts bare and not a few of them frisked around, enjoying the fact that the men were watching their firm young breasts.

Randell looked at him hard. "Stan, don't use that tone of voice at me unless you want me to return the compliment. We'll let the contract speak for itself."

Moose snapped at Stan. "Say, Stan, you know how I feel about you? *This* is how I feel about you." He held his nose between his fingers like he smelled some nasty, funky odor, and then with his other hand he pulled down on an imaginary chain of a lavatory.

Moose could be funny at times, he really could. While I suppressed my laughter, Fran returned with his briefcase.

Kingsley turned to Randell with his ass on his face. "Why

didn't somebody tell you you were being cheated?" he asked.

"Didn't anybody *know* he was being cheated," Clea said. So far, the biggest lie of the day.

Randell stormed off the set. He was hurt. When Moose saw how hurt he was his blood started boiling in his skin.

"I read the original script Randell wrote," Moose stammered. "And you've fucked it up. You spend a million dollars on this damn set and then fuck up the script. Where are the good scenes Randell gave the slaves? The slaves have to have more lines!"

Stan Krass was holding a copy of Thomas Jefferson's *Notes on the State of Virginia,* a prop, in his hand.

"This is my film, buster," he said, shaking the prop in Moose's face. "And if you don't like the way it's being shot, get off the set! We got a movie to shoot, buddy."

Moose grabbed the book and snatched it out of Mr. Krass's hand and popped him on the head with it. "Now what do you think of that?" he asked Mr. Krass imprudently.

Mr. Krass turned and started to walk away. Moose grabbed him by the neck. "Is this the way you want me to choke him!" he yelled to Kingsley.

The actor playing M. Hugo Baptiste, the dancing master, took his three-corner hat off and hit Moose across the head with it.

"Stop that! Stop this insanity!" he shouted. But before he knew it the black actor playing the role of slave conspirator General John grabbed him from behind and threw him against the whipping post. Then another white actor, who played Alexander Budenburst, the printer, came to Krass's rescue, but when Solomon, one of the black actors, saw this he jumped in front of him with a riding whip in his hand and began to flay him with it on his backside. Then the white extras playing the quality white folks clashed with the black extras playing the slaves and began to tear into each other. (I mean, it was something to watch, Jim.)

That sepia actress Cynthia Bell, who played Melody, the mulatto slave girl, pulled up her leaf-green petticoat and ran across the set into the Dirty Spoon, but Jewel riding Araby, that young stallion, cut her off before she could make it and slapped her back down to the ground with a riding crop.

"I told ya to give me some more lines, motherfucker," Moose was screaming. "I WANT SOME MORE LINES! A SLAVE GOT TO HAVE PLENTY TO SAY!"

"Slave revolt! Slave revolt in Democracy!" the black extras were yelling. "Tear the sucker down! Burn, baby, burn!"

Standing on the catwalk, Tull aimed a prop for a white actor's head beneath him. Little Eva ran to Mr. Prosser, the slave master, but Uncle Tom grabbed him by his head and douched him in the water trough.

Moose chased Kingsley and caught him. "You damn house nigger," he shouted into his face and drew back a fist and let him have it. Kingsley staggered off and fell over his fat script girl, who was screaming, "Help! Help! Help!"

Kingsley screamed back, "Will you shut up! It's only a movie!"

"I always knew you were an Uncle Tom director," Moose yelled to him. "You white man's boy!"

From the catwalk Tull was pouring the blackish liquid blood from a vat down on the heads of the fighting white actors.

Some black birds flew over the set and a thundercloud burst and it began to rain—except, it was just a rain machine at work, not God.

I saw Mr. Grayeye then was behind the camera with the cameraman. "Shoot!" he commanded. "Shoot it! It's marvelous! *Shoot it!*"

What he was doing, he was shooting the revolt. In the

confusion people were running every which way to get out of the way of the revolting slaves.

"Oh, my lord, that chile!" I heard the Uncle Tom screaming, and I looked down and saw Little Eva bobbing up and down in the water beside the steamboat. "SAVE THE CHILE!" he said and leaped off the steamboat. Forgetting his role, he swam out to save her.

The cameraman was following Mr. Grayeye III's impatient command: "Shoot it! Shoot! Shoot!"

While Uncle Tom saved Little Eva, these other actors were trashing the whole damn set, what Mr. Grayeye III was doing was directing the cameraman where to shoot.

The fake rain was coming down fast and the thunder machine clapping loud and the extras playing the slaves were yelling and carrying on and the extras playing the slave masters and their crew were just screaming and birds were flying all over the goddamn place and that goddamn tempestuous brown wench Jewel was galloping that Araby all over the goddamn set and her brown thighs were clutching to that young colt and she was just riding her ass off and Mr. Grayeye was screaming with a fool's delight at the cameraman, *"Shoot! Shoot! Shoot* the goddamn picture!"—whew! Well, it was something.

When it all quieted down, Mr. Grayeye he got up and gave this speech about how well everybody acted and how proud he was of them. But at first they all looked at him like he was crazy. He said, "I've always dreamed of shooting a scene like that!" and that everybody was going to get a big bonus because of the way they acted. Moose said, "Acting, my ass! We were serious!" Mr. Grayeye said, "Whatever technique you used is your own business! All I know is that I've gotten the best footage I've ever gotten on camera! We have a big hit this time!"

When I left, Moose was shaking the other actors' hands and they shook his hands and they all congratulated each other on their performances. Jewel got down off the horse and told everybody how she enjoyed playing her part and they all told each other that they were only acting. Actors are big phonies any goddamn way. To tell you the truth, I didn't feel too bad about not being in this film.

# 27

I found Clea in her office.

"I'm embarrassed and ashamed of what happened to our script. I thought you were on my side."

"Well, so I am." She shrugged. (I could see the cold side of her emerging. Now I saw she'd been lying to me and all she wanted was the power of having produced this movie. She didn't give a damn about what was in it.)

"We can fight Grayeye, Clea. If you love me, you'll help me fight him. We've got to do it."

She picked up a cigarette and turned her back to me, and faced the view of the back lot. Farther out in the distance we could see the camera crew struggling against the hills like mere ants.

"No, we can't do that," she said.

I lit her cigarette. "I want you to prove to me what you said when we first met. You said you believed in making quality pictures and not exploitation pictures. By letting Grayeye sneak in scenes from *Uncle Tom's Cabin* and *Middle Passage,* we are allowing them to exploit a good film script! If we fail in this, other film companies in the future will have failed, too! Don't you see that?"

She turned and faced me sharply. "So I broke my promise?"

"Yes, you did. And you lied to Randell. You told him he would get another ten thousand when the film began, and you changed his script! Now you say he didn't contribute to the final draft! Just pay him, Clea! You know if it wasn't for him you wouldn't even be *making* the film. He got you off the hook with those women groups! Just pay the guy!"

"What is this with Randell? What do you care about him? You're going to get credit for this film, so why're you worried about him?"

"Because—" How do you explain to somebody something when you yourself don't understand it. I wanted to say to her that Randell was a real writer and not a hack like my uncle, and I wanted to tell her that in the black community a real writer was worth a million white writers. I wanted to tell her that Randell was a visionary poet even though I was not quite sure what a visionary poet was, to tell the truth, but I knew he was serious and that was enough for me.

Clea didn't say anything but I could tell I'd gotten to her. She'd met Randell and she liked him, but she had become too callous to admit to her feelings.

"You'll have your money and your credit. It's no damn skin off your teeth," she said. "Jonah, you're young. You're going to be a star, baby. On your next picture, you'll be able to do all those things you wanted to do on this one."

"That's the biggest lie ever told in this business," I said. "Nobody ever gets to do the film he wants to do. It's a myth. Just like the one about the Nielsen ratings. The highest Nielsen ratings will be on the day the Russians drop that nuclear bomb on us. Except, there won't be anybody here to watch the show. It's up to us to decide what is more important, our feelings for one another as human beings or some goddamn rating system and some myths. I don't wanna hear this crap from you. You're a woman, so you're suppose to be sensitive to what blacks need."

She chopped the air with her hands like somebody hacking his way out of a suffocating jungle. "Just because I'm a woman, I'm suppose to be emotional?" she said. "Don't you see this is as much a stereotype as slaves are for blacks? I want to *cut* through that prison. And this position has helped me do that. It really has, Jonah. And I thank all the black people on *Black Thunder* that have helped me discover my true self-assertiveness. It's really hard having to keep up the image of being a white woman in a position over so many black films. Jonah, you're black. You understand, don't you?"

"Yes, I understand." What I wanted to do was just reach over that desk and smack her good. She'd be all right if somebody just smacked her good two or three times a day.

"And besides," she said, now looking out the window at the film crew, "we did make *some* progress in this film."

"Oh?"

"Yes, there's only *one* lesbian scene in this film," she said. "And only *some* of the slaves are happy."

"How could this studio spend a million dollars on the plantation set design and then throw out a genuine script, only to hire a couple of hacks like my uncle and Victor Klingentight. How?"

"Because the man who runs the studio is not only stupid but greedy and ignorant as well. He's a tyrant and he has ultimate power," she said. "Also, it's safe. We must keep a white sheet over the public's head. That way, we make money and they buy our myths of white supremacy. My ambition is to make black films that whites will buy. I will become rich. Then people will respect me." She turned to face me and held her hands out to me like an imploring beggar. "Jonah, you can join me. I *beg* you to. Let's make money *together*. If you're rich, who cares if you're black. Look at all the black celebrities in this town. They're rich and famous. Everybody treats them just like they're white. Don't hold back, Jonah. Join me! When you have a long list of credits, the studio will love you, everybody will love you! Look at Billy Badman. He's rich and famous and everybody loves him! You can do the same thing!"

I thought to myself, this bitch has flipped out completely. *Gadge was right,* I thought. *They are in it for the money!* In that parking lot behind the Comedy Club, Gadge had told me white people were not interested in the truth. He had been right. I was a fool. A victim of the same system that had exploited me, Clea had been forced to betray me and the other blacks just like the house niggers Tom and Pharoah had betrayed Gabriel Prosser.

"I've quit the mailroom a while ago," I reminded her. "I guess I'll go back to comedy."

"Hello?" somebody said at the door.

"Come in," Clea called. The door opened and a young brother entered. He couldn't've been more than twenty. He carried the leather mailbag on his shoulders and he was wearing my old uniform I'd inherited from Major.

"Good morning, Mrs. Menchan," he said, all very cheerfully.

"Good morning, Cootie," Clea said. "Cootie, this is Mr. Drinkwater. He started as a mailboy here and rose to the level of associate producer."

"Gee-whiz! Gosh darn! Really?" Cootie said all excited. He kept glancing, looking at me, though I caught the little bastard's eyes glancing at Clea's legs on the sly. My uniform was too big for him, to tell you the truth.

"Cootie, Mr. Drinkwater is a well-known comedian. Would you like to join me tonight to see him perform?"

How easily she praised me, how easy it was for them to say we have genius!

"Oh, yes, Mrs. Menchan! I really would like that!" Cootie Yes Ma'amed like a black robot.

"Good! Then pick me up at my house at eight," Clea said. "And we can have dinner and discuss your screenplay." She turned to me and said, "Cootie wants to be a writer."

His screenplay—ho, ho.

Cootie acknowledged his ambition with a smile and bolted for the door.

"And, Cootie," I said, "let me give you a tip. There's a place on Santa Monica called Jim's Tailor. Jim's a friend of mine. Take the uniform in and tell him to take in about two inches in the shoulders. It'll feel snugly on your shoulders and it'll also improve your appearance."

He smiled and said, "Thank you." He sort of bowed his head into my direction and went out the door.

"Ain't he sweet and so cute?" Clea said, lighting up a cigarette.

"The only thing cuter than Cootie," I said sardonically, "is you, Mrs. Menchan!" I wanted to laugh, I really did. Where did they find Cootie? "Did you say you're bringing Cootie to my performance tonight?"

"Oh yes!" she said. "I think it'll be wonderful to take him out. You just can't imagine how naïve he is!"

"So what'd you do with old Cootie? Tell him that *Black Thunder* wasn't *black* enough? Tell him that his script is the *real* black script? Use him like you used me and go on to the next one?"

"See? You're getting bitter," she said, shaking her finger in my face. "I've warned you about that."

"Whatcha gonna do, then? Clea, if you keep getting these small mailboys, pretty soon the uniform is going to be large enough for a midget." I turned to the door. "You got a nice thing going, baby." I shook my finger in *her* face. "As a friend, I tell you, don't bring that little, ugly, monkey-face sucker to my performance tonight. You will regret it."

"Jonah, my God, you're something like a foaming-at-the-mouth racist. Let's get one thing straight. What we had together was fun. You were never in love with me and I was never in love with you. Let's be straight about that. You have no right to tell me where to go and where not to go."

I opened the door and stood in it. "How would you know what my feelings were? You were too busy trying to make this deal to ask. But I am warning you—don't bring that simpleton to my performance."

I walked out the door and slammed it.

# 28

AS soon as I left the studio I went home and knocked on Randell's door. When he opened the door he looked dazed.

"Come in, blood," he said and I went in.

I saw the glass pipes on the table.

"Say, man, what you doin'?" I was pissed. He looked like he was freebasing.

"Basin'," he said, and that really hurt me.

He went over to the stove and lifted the vial of cocaine that was heating up in the pan. He shook the bottle so that the liquid contents turned milky gray. He shook it again and put it back in the pan, and looked at me, smiled, and rubbed his hands together vigorously.

"It'll be ready in a minute," he said. "You want some base?"

I was pretty pissed, I can tell you. He was cooking his own brain in that pan.

"No," I said. "You go on, man. I just don't think you should do it. Isn't this what you accused Trudy of doing?"

He sat down and picked up a pack of cigarettes. When he struck the match to light the cigarette, I noticed for the first time the panic in his swollen and puffy face. Bleary, his eyes had retreated behind hooded, inscrutable brows.

"I like you, Jonah, because we can talk," he said tonelessly and emotionally. "We're friends."

"Yes," I said.

"Trudy couldn't go the distance," he said. "But you have

to remember that a black woman with her background, and her fame, is in love with whites. Hollywood really does exist for Trudy. She has had a lot to escape from. And Hollywood is a very convenient place to escape to. A refuge."

"Yes, but what about you?"

He got up and went to the stove and held the cocaine up to the light. He shook it in the light, and then opened the vial.

"What about me?" he asked.

He took some of the cocaine out of the vial with a pair of tweezers and placed it on a dry paper towel.

He folded the edge of the napkin over the cocaine and rubbed it between his fingers.

He put the tiny ball of freebase on the screen of the water pipe and struck a cigarette lighter against it. Gradually he sucked in with air through the pipe and the flame caused the freebase to melt. A white cloud gathered in the bottom of the pipe for a moment, and then disappeared as Randell drew it into his lungs.

He spared me the temptation by not offering the pipe in my direction, but instead set it on the table.

I watched him as he released his breath, coughed, and then hit his chest with his fist. His eyes bulged, and he kept coughing terribly.

"They turned the black man's tragedy into a comedy," he said. "What's left for me to do but kill myself?"

"Look, you've got to stop this," I said. "It's not the worst thing a writer could do."

"When my friends in Berkeley see this film they will laugh at me. I gave up my teaching job to do this? To prostitute myself, my history, my talent?" he asked. "Are you kidding? Death would be the only dignified way out!"

"Look, if you get a chance," I told him, "come by the club. I'll try to make you laugh."

He went back to the base pipe.

# 29

"WELL, you're just a comic to them. They exploit you at the studio, but now they're in the mood for a laugh, you're suppose to make them laugh," Prufrock said. "Oh, by the way, I have something to tell you. Did you hear about your friend Randell?"

"What?" I asked him. We were back at Ben Frank's.

"Oh, you didn't hear? Well, I hate to be the one to bring you bad news," he said, "but I think he was in an accident."

"What happened?"

Prufrock said, "He's in the hospital, if you want to see him. Robin came by and told me to tell you he was in the hospital. I don't know the details but it's Cedars-Sinai."

I jumped up.

Prufrock always exaggerated hearsay, yet I wondered if Randell was dead. I just couldn't believe it. I had just seen him a couple of hours ago! Yet I knew, as I ran desperately to the door, that it was true. I had just seen him at the apartment, and he looked very depressed, but I didn't think he would kill himself. Now he was in the hospital—dead or alive, I didn't know.

I got in a taxi at the newspaper stand and told him to take me to the Cedars-Sinai Hospital. All the way there, I went over final details about Randell's life. Where would the body be sent? Who were his parents? Didn't he tell us he was from Detroit? Moose would know all this. Where was Moose? Randell dead? I couldn't believe it.

"This is it, buddy," the driver said, bringing the cab to a

halt. Having paid him, I opened the door and scrambled out into a sheet of rain.

The nurse at the information desk told me to go to the third floor.

Just as I was coming off the elevator, I saw Randell. He was all right.

"She's dead," he sobbed.

"Who?"

"Trudy," he said, crying.

It was true. He told me the whole story. During a performance at The Roxie, Gertrude Williams, the soul singer turned disco, fell dead from a heart attack in the middle of her act.

That night, Thalia came over to my table at the Comedy Club. "Jonah," she said, "there's somebody to see you."

"Who?" I asked. I was half hoping it would be Randell.

"I think it's your uncle," she said.

I went into the main room. Sure enough, old Gadge and his babe were sitting at one of the tables over in the corner. They were laughing at Prufrock, who was on stage joking them about horror films.

I went over and patted him on the shoulder. He looked up and smiled. "Say, Gadge," I said, "how you doin'?"

"Jonah! Jonah! How you been, boy," he said. "You know Mortimer, don'tcha?"

It was dark and at first I didn't recognize the other people at his table. I almost flipped my wig, though, when I saw it was Clea Menchan, Cootie, and Mr. Grayeye.

"How have you been, Jonah, old boy," Mr. Grayeye said. "We miss you out on the lot."

I looked over and saw Clea Menchan. It was dark but I could tell she was staring at me. Then I felt her hand on mine. I quietly removed my hand from the table.

"Sit down, boy," Uncle Gadge said.

"No, thank you," I said. "I've got to go on soon."

"I asked you not to come tonight," I told Clea. "Get out!"

"Oh, Jonah, I'm so excited to see you perform at last," she said.

"Every promise you've made to me, you've broken," I said. "Don't you think I got any pride?"

"But why are you still harping on that issue?" she asked. "The film is finished now."

"Okay, I'll go on," I told her and she started smiling. "But all of you, Mr. Grayeye, and Gadge, and that damn Cootie—you tell them they gotta keep quiet. I don't want them even in here, in the first place, but now that they're here, what can I do? Just tell them if they get outa line, that's it—I'm coming after them. You heard me?"

"Okay," she said. "Just be good. Don't get any crazy ideas, and you know what I'm talking about."

When I got back to my table, Thalia asked me if I wanted to go on, did I feel up to it. I thought it was very considerate of her but I told her I was all right. But I was a little late getting on the stage.

As I came up on the stage, some lady pointed that out: "He's late." When I got to the mike, I looked at my watch.

"Yeah, you're right. I'm late again. Does anybody know why black people are always late? Why? Because there's never enough time? Yeah—I agree. We never have time, do we? I guess that's why we have *timing* . . .*!*"

I paused and caught a few laughs with that. "But you know, being slow is an advantage sometimes. For example, Mr. Snail's wife took sick. Mrs. Snail wasn't feeling well. That's right—she'd gone out that night and eaten some escargots. She sent her husband to get a doctor. Well, about *seven* years *later* she heard a noise at the door. She said, 'Thank you, honey, for getting the doctor.' Mr. Snail said, 'Woman, don't rush me! I'm just gettin' to de *do'* to *git* dat doctor!'"

I kept my eyes on old Clea. She hadn't looked at Cootie yet. She kept her eyes riveted on me. And Cootie kept laughing at me; he hadn't looked at her yet.

Just looking at Clea brought to my mind Randell's misery. How strange that we can cause so much pain to other people and not care at all? Her image whispered mockingly at my own self-doubt, and laughed at Lindsey's murder. It all came to me in a flash. What I'll do, I'll at least make fun of her, I decided. No, bitch, you won't be so cool when I'm finished with you.

Then I turned to the audience, speaking in an entirely different tone of voice.

"Ladies and gents," I said, "we have some celebrities here tonight. Seated over there in the back are King Kong and Fay Wray!" I pointed to Clea and Cootie. The house gasped then, and had a good gratifying chuckle.

"I know that's a little racial slur on my own people, but you know I really don't give a shit. But I was just kiddin'. Ha, ha, ha!" Clea looked at me as if she was about to say, "Are you talking to me?"

Encouraged by the huge reward the audience gave me for that joke on Clea and her little black-ass simp, I suddenly got a flash of insight on a bit about King Kong and Fay Wray.

I skipped all of my own routines and just did free-flowing ad-lib as it happened. I wanted to strike out and hit them, wake them up to reality.

I stood there smoking the cigarette with one hand on the mike, my eyes gunning Clea's table. I took another drag and said, "Wouldn't it be funny if Barbara Walters *did* one of those interviews she always does on people—you know, if she did one on King Kong and Fay Wray." I saw Tull and Buddy chuckle. Prufrock bent over and beat his knees and flashed his teeth.

"That's right, folks! Barbara Walters goes to visit that well-known couple King Kong and his girlfriend at *their* spacious Hollywood mansion in the secluded section of Benedict Canyon. Can't you just see the scene? The camera cuts to this big mansion, right? You see the Mercedes and the Rolls-Royce in the carport, you see the black maid, you see the whole bourgeois lay-out . . ." And I started describing Clea's house in detail. She laughed because she knew exactly what I was talking about. ". . . and then and then you see Barbara herself at the front door, right? . . . they're just lying back on the sofa and King Kong has his big gigantic *cock* in his hand . . . and what a *cock* it is! Ten feet long and three feet wide and poor Fay Wray is struggling with it, poor girl, trying to stuff it up her *snatch* . . . and Barbara is looking embarrassed, right? But she's a good journalist . . . she's determined to go through with this incredible scene, right? . . . She's sticking the microphone right up into Fay Wray's mouth, right? . . . 'Well, tell our viewers out there, Fay, how does it feel to be living with such a legend?' Fay is just sweating like hell trying to get this huge thing in her twat, right? But she's a good girl and she wants to go on with this thing, too.

"Fay is going, *'Oh, God! Monster! A little to the right, Monster! Ahhhaaaahhh-aaa! Monster! Ah, King, do it to me, Big Kong! Ah, shit, Big Boy! To the left, Big Black Nigger! To the left, you shithead! Shoot that quart of come in me, you big* BLACK PUMPKIN!' "

Uncle Gadge tried to help her out by laughing very loudly.

"We don't like to be teased, do we?" I said to them. "We're really scared of the truth, aren't we?"

"Be careful, son," Uncle Gadge said. "Be careful . . . You may never work in this town again."

"Oh, by the way, ladies and gents, that's my uncle over there," I joked. "He's a pretty fat cat now. He doesn't like me to say anything about how he *is making* it in this town. He makes a good two hundred thousand a year writing stereotypes that whites want to see. But *he* doesn't want anybody else to know it. And why? He wants to be the only *black* screenwriter in Hollywood. Not only is he greedy, but he is also envious. If a black writer of talent comes along, my uncle will be the first to tell the whites that he's a terrorist. Anything to get him out of the competition. Oh, he hates me for saying this. Just look at him now. *'Jonah, you'll never work in this town again!'* Well, I got news for all of you motherfuckers out there. I DON'T WANT TO WORK IN THIS TOWN AGAIN! Is that clear, you assholes?" Then I shuffled and said, "Just kiddin'. Ha! Ha! Ha!"

Covering his face with his glass, Gadge pretended to belly-laugh at what I'd said. The audience started booing me, though, and I turned against me, too.

Then I went too far. I allowed the audience to get to me.

"What? Are you still there?" I snarled at them. "I had forgotten about you. You stupid assholes who pay good money to see a nigger in a zoo, isn't that right?"

"Fuck you!" somebody heckled.

Wonderful. It made me feel wonderful and proud of myself.

"Oh, yes," I tortured them. "You want me to stand up here and heap abuses on you. Call you white racist motherfuckers, don'tcha?"

"You're so preoccupied about racism, mister? Are you sure you're not a racist yourself?" A heavyset white lady belly-laughed.

"See? I like her." I picked at them. "She admits she's a racist—at least, she's honest. You wanna see a crazy-jiveass nigger, don'tcha?"

"Screw you, buster!" A guy stood up and hurled the insult at me.

". . . You want a Gabriel Prosser? . . . Nat *Turner?* Would that be crazy enough for you? You need me to tell you how fucked up you are . . . Well, I'm fucked up too! So fuck you!"

That was a twist! Then I did a stupid thing. I started

downstage and tripped over the mike cord. Somebody laughed. "He's drunk!"

"No, I'm not drunk."

"Tell a joke, then, fool—" a sister girl yelled. "I want my money's worth!"

"What do you take me for, young lady?" I asked her. "A comedian? A clown? A fool? Am I a comic? No—no . . . I'm a damn *fool*. I wish I was a real comedian. I've been up on this stage to be one. Oh, God—give me the strength—for a moment only—to be a great comic! See? Nothing happened." I made a violent gesture like I was trying to rip open my chest.

"See? Nothing! I am just another fucked-over black comic. Why can't I be a great comedian? I'm a failure. All against me? All at once? But lemme ask you a question? What have I DONE to you, you dumb shits. You dumb fucks. These people are the ones you should be angry with."

I pointed to Gadge, Clea, and Mortimer Grayeye III's table.

"Basically they are nice people but don't come down on me, because I'm just tryin' to be funny. They are motivators! Heh, heh, heh!" I shuffled like Stepin Fetchit. People who got it started laughing. People who didn't get it yelled back, "Fuck you! Shitface!"

"Oh, I thought you loved me." I laughed. "You don't love me? Oh, I see!—you think I'm funny if I tell you jokes, but *not* funny if I tell the truth? Well, who needs an audience like you, anyway?"

Turning my back on them, I lighted another cigarette.

"And who needs you, shitface!" somebody else yelled back.

"You do! You want an illusion. That's why I'm up here and you're down there, you weak-ass half-alive voyeurs—! Ha, ha, ha!" I laughed at them as I did my shuffle again.

"Throw Jonah overboard," another one shouted. By this time the heckling had grown louder and I heard Uncle Gadge's voice among them.

Uncle Gadge had stood up and was having a great time as he shook his finger at me. He was the comic now!

"This boy was always a lazy, no-damn-good scoundrel! And he still ain't funny!"

Led by my uncle, the audience congratulated itself on its humor. Uncle Gadge was talking to them about me, and getting laughs. "He was sick as a child, and we didn't think he'd live, but he did live. He WAS never right in the head, and there is nothing wrong with him now that a psychiatrist and some of those wonder drugs like Compazine and Mellaril wouldn't cure! He's a sick, degenerate, PSYCHOTIC, BLACK SONOVABITCH! I'LL KILL HIM! NIGGER, STOP TELLING THESE WHITE PEOPLE YOU AND MINE'S PERSONAL SECRETS FOR SUCCESS IN THIS WHITE GREAT WHITE WORLD!"

I was so proud my uncle had the guts to get that angry. Isn't that what Stubbs said? "When it comes to you, you'll know it." My God, it had happened to me, I'd found myself! No, really. "FUCK YOU PEOPLE!" I screamed at them. "You want somebody crazy? Ok-KAY-ee!"

"FUCK YOU!" they screamed back at me.

Just then I decided I'd moon them and just as I decided against it, a man standing on the table pulled down his pants and bared his white ass.

"HERE, NIGGER, KISS IT!" He laughed. "KISS IT!"

At the next table Thelma Jackson, the famous black comedian, sat with her white date. This black bitch screamed about niggers going out with white women, and every time you saw her she was with a white boy. With a mink fur thrown around her shoulders (and in that hot weather, too), she snuggled closer to her white gigolo. Realizing how she made herself rich by playing a black female mamma in a TV situation comedy, I lashed out at the vice she personified.

"And you, black bitch?" I snarled at her. "And stop looking at that white man like you don't know what I mean. All the niggers in Hollywood know about you and your drug habit. Send your children to school, bitch, and stop buying yourself an early grave with that freebase. Then, on the other hand . . . hahhaha! I'm just a simple fool."

"Oh, he's so funny, isn't he?" she said out loud, trying to laugh it off. "What a genius . . . !"

"Genius my ass, I'll tell you something else, a fool can speak the truth, because he can get away with it. And—"

"You're sick, asshole, sit down!"

"You sit down, this is my act, get your own!"

"You're a sick egghead with maggots on the brain!"

Was my uncle the father of that wonderful execration? I sure hoped so. Now there were so many.

Despite the confusion, it was time for me to answer the accusations. "Yeah, I'm sick, but if I am, you made me sick. If I'm a jiveass nigger, you made me one . . . Jonah is not here . . . He died a long time ago. You, the public, made me into an asshole, a Bigger Thomas, an Uncle Tom, a Stepin Fetchit, so ha, ha, ha! and kiss my black ass! Just kiddin'. Goodnight, folks!"

They didn't know what to think.

"You fake!" somebody yelled.

"You con art-artist!" Uncle Gadge yelled.

"Get off the stage!"

Somebody threw a chair on the stage. Well, I threw the chair *back!* "Take that, you assholes!"

"You crazy, boy, you crazy!" Uncle Gadge shouted out at me, and threw his glass at me. He had such a lousy aim that the glass missed me about a mile and shattered on the wall behind me.

"Oh, is that you again, Gadge?" I jeered him. "Listen, Uncle Tom, I'll kick your ass. Why don't you put a tombstone on your own brother's grave with all the money you rip off from these whites, you scum! Oh, excuse me, ladies and gentlemen—but we're closing the club up."

We sure were closing it up, too—another chair landed up at my feet, though it was aimed for my head.

The audience formed their troops into a battle formation and prepared for a major operation, led by Pompous Gadge. Their battle cry was: "It ain't white! We want our money back!" Next to him stood the deceitful, ambitious Clea Menchan cleaving a chair rung. With a grim brow, she meant to kill any comic who exposed her. Standing next to her was her cohort Cootie with his slingshot made from strips of red-checked oilcloth. But behind them were the horrendous Hackneyed Hecklers, which consisted of specialized hecklers, the Fag Heckler, the Black Heckler, the Indian Heckler, the Yellow Peril Heckler, the Female Heckler. All armed to the teeth with deadly pieces of chair and table. You could tell their rank by what piece of furniture they carried. Only the very best of their group could carry table legs. Behind them was Big Black Thelma Johnson armed with a black skillet no doubt inherited from Louise Beaver.

Bellicose, saber rattling, they rushed forward meaning to instill fear among our ranks of Comedy and Camp, our comedies were ranked as Dark, Light, High, Low, and our Camp —as Camp, High Camp, and Low Camp.

But like our enemy, we were armed to the T. The Throat-Slitting Wit Prufrock, wielding a table leg like it was a switchblade, was in command of High Camp troops. Subtle-Witted Buddy, captain of the Low Camp troops, swooped down on them with a chair leg. Master of Buffoonery Fatso Mitchell, commanding the Slapstick Section, flew into the midst of the fray with a chair; Mr. Straight Comic Jack White, leader of the Genteel Comedy, dashed into the scuffle, whipping heads with a piece of the stage door. Indian Comic Charlie Horse went on the warpath with a chair rung that he wielded like a tomahawk; Gilbert Wong, the leader of Slant-Eyed Humor, pounced on the enemy with a table leg, which the enemy thought was a samurai sword; lesbian co-median Robbin led the comic Lesbos of Transsexual Tickles with a candleholder and the audience declared war. "You comics are lousy! We can do better!"

Invisible, the Goddess and Gods of war swoomed through the air. Fame rushed over to Thalia for protection. The Battle of Comedy was on.

The comics let slip the dogs of war. Their battle cry, "Fuck you, assholes!"

"Geronimo!" Charlie Horse aimed a tomahawk blow to the head of the Yellow Peril Heckler, but the blow deflected from the hard head of this dull-humored creature. Meanwhile, an Out-of-Towner caught one of the comics with an uppercut that left the poor fellow bellyaching. Taking revenge for their fallen compatriot, the High Camp comics scattered the ranks of Hecklers. Clea was no match for the wit of Switch-blade Prufrock. Her chair leg missed its mark and the switchblade would've cut her to ribbons had not Athena, invisible, replaced her skirt with the tablecloth; Fatso Mitch-ell would've broadaxed Cootie to death had not Wotan, invis-ible, replaced his head with an ashtray. Uncle Gadge rushed to the bar and ordered drinks for his entire troops—what was left of them, that is—and Thalia granted that the Battle of Comedy was profitable indeed. A Heckler found a target right in Gilbert Wong's left, slanted eye, but Minerva made him move his head just in time. The chair leg flew out through the plate-glass window.

One of the comics hit one of the black girls in the eye and she hauled off and popped him upside his head. Her boy-friend, a six-footer, started beating the white comic's ass.

I ducked behind the black curtain that hung behind the stage and eluded them. When I came out the other side, I could see the audience tearing the place up and throwing everything it could get its hands on at the comics. I headed for the back door, but three-hundred-pound Thelma Johnson, that black bitch of a comedian, blocked my exit.

"Stand back!" I warned her. She stood back and threw up her dukes like a man.

"Well, come on, bitch," I said and smacked her good upside the head. She fell backwards and landed square on her ass. I'd knocked that ugly broad down.

"The next time you won't jump in a man's face, hussy!" I told her. Pissed me off.

Thelma was still sprawled out.

When I got outside, I discovered it was pouring down rain.

"There he is!" Fatso yelled after me.

"Get him!!" yelled Jack White coming outside.

"He's gettin' away!"

"Jonah! Wait! I got something for you," Prufrock said, but I pulled out and left them all behind.

Parking my car, I jumped out onto the street. Boy, was it raining! Gushes of water rolled down the streets and trees bent under the pressure of the wind, as I ran up Sunset. A whore ran across my path like a chicken in a thunderstorm. Water ran everywhere. I made a dash for Ben Franks. Angry black clouds hung overhead.

# 30

**I**'M going, I thought to myself even before I'd realized it, South. Back to the good old South. No more of this.

My nightly nightmare was over. For the first time in my life, I'd enjoyed being an artist. For the first time, I'd *felt* like an artist. I didn't need anybody to tell me.

"Lordy! You sho' soaking wet!"

I looked up and saw Lois slide a hot cup of coffee under my face. Just then an angry cloud burst and the dagger points of the rain plummeted into the roof, sounding like the portentous death roll on snare drums. When I ran from the club, my feet had instinctively taken me there.

"You better try get outa those soaking clothes, before you catch a cold worsen then the one you got."

But I wasn't listening to her. I looked around. Not a single Hollywood Wit in sight. Now that I've found myself, not a goddamn soul in sight to celebrate.

Drinking my coffee, listening to the rain outside, seeing the variegated humanity come through the swinging doors of that all-night diner, I quietly gave my prayers up to God for this insight: *I'm gonna make it, I'm not going to be just another anonymous, obscure, undistinguished, and undifferentiated nigger. No, I'm going to be famous. Everybody's gonna know my name. They gonna know I am one of God's creatures, too.* That I wanted to return to the South now that I was sure of not just being another statistic didn't seem odd to me at all: I had been confirmed in a conviction about myself, and could now go home. The whale of experience had delivered me on the sandy shore of Nineveh at last.

"I've got to pack," I heard myself say.

"All the roads closed, chile," Lois said. "These white people ain't ready for no storm in Hollywood, I'm tellin' ya. Houses falling down off the hills in Malibu Canyon, did you hear about that? People are dying in this storm. Cars are floating down Sunset Boulevard. It's a . . ."

Say it, I thought, say Black Thunder.

". . . disaster area," Lois went on. The place was practically empty, save me and some lonely-looking guy sitting in the corner. I looked at him again and recognized Randell.

He looked weathered, like a cock that had just come in out of the rain. He must be feeling like Gabriel Prosser, I thought, after his defeat.

"Sit down," he greeted me. He was having tea, and a copy of *Variety* was spread out across the table.

"All the roads are closed going north," I explained. "But the roads going south are open."

"Did you see *Variety?*" he asked, and held up the paper. "That film is gonna be a hit. Already some reporter says it will be the most controversial film of the year."

"What film—*Black Thunder?*"

"Yes."

As fate would have it, Randell was right. A few months after the picture was released, people were breaking down the doors to see it. Critics thought it was a surrealistic parody of *Roots. The New Yorker* described it as a "bizarre black-humor masterpiece." It broke all records by earning eight million dollars in the first three days. Some experts say it was because of Billy Badman's appearance. Others, knowing the business better, pointed to the "Grayeye III touch." I have my own theory.

"Well, how do you feel about it? You're going to have money again."

"I feel terrible is how I feel. Here I am, a good writer, and now here I am again, a rich writer, but they didn't even use my good script! How can I explain that to myself?"

"But you're going to be rich," I said. "Of course, I know it will be difficult to accept, but you'll get use to it. And what about Ritual now? How do you feel about that experience?"

"She was just that—a ritual bondage that I had to live through. She is the City herself. The same old paralyzing routine, the same old shit. Now that she's dead, I am free."

"Do you still like her music?"

"It's the music of the city, isn't it?"

I didn't feel sorry for him any more.

Then I saw Buddy coming in.

"You knocked them dead." He laughed. "Your name will be in all the papers tomorrow. You insulted some of the most famous people in Hollywood."

"Sit down and shut up," I told him. "Do you two know each other? No? Then, Randell, this is Buddy."

But then Prufrock came in and sat down. He was all up in my face, too. "You made a hit tonight, Homeboy. You made a statement. You spoke from your heart, you said a lot of things people wanted to say themselves but couldn't. You said it for them! You personally spoke for me, too!"

*Speaking from my heart!* I had to admit he had me there. What could I say? Was there anywhere else to speak the truth from? But he wasn't finished, and I had to sit there while he went on with this speech.

"You found yourself tonight, too," he went on. "You *discovered* yourself."

"Oh, I did, huh? Suppose you tell me who I am then?"

"You're a very *angry* and *sick* and *disturbed* person, but you're *honest.* People *believe* you when you speak. Because they see the pain in your face and feel it in your voice: that's the truth! There is so much *pain* in you!"

"In other words," Prufrock said, "you've arrived at a stage

presence. You've begun to accept yourself the way they see you. The public will now expect this anger from you. You can now be rich and famous." He laughed ironically. "But don't worry, we won't tell the world you happened on it by accident!"

"But I meant it! I *am* angry!" I told them. "But right now I want some sleep."

"Hahahaha!" Buddy laughed.

"What's so damn funny?"

"You!" He laughed, and everybody laughed.

"But what about Thalia? We messed her place up pretty bad, didn't we?" I asked.

"Oh, she doesn't care," Buddy said. "She's only thinking of all the publicity she's getting from your scandal."

"I know. . . . How did they react to what I said?"

"Oh, they thought you were terrific! Producers are interested in promoting your career," Prufrock said. "Listen, you spoke the truth. They have to make you famous now. That's how Hollywood deals with the truth. Insults are greeted with laughter. They make you so famous that nobody'll take you serious any more. They will expect it from you now. It's the paradox of success!"

"But I meant it! I meant it! Don'tcha see!" I screamed at them. But everybody just laughed at me.

They had caught me. They really had. Jonah, I had to tell myself, they really got you this time. What I'll do, I told myself, I'll use this money to help get my ass back to Georgia. Buy myself some land and do some farming. I could just picture myself on my own farm. Just living life and having a good time with my honest friends. And never going to a movie.

The next thing I knew, I was walking down the street, with the rain in my face. There was a king who was told by his soothsayers that a big rain was coming. But that if anybody drank the rainwater they would go mad. So the king gathered up fresh water for himself. The rain came and all of his subjects drank it and became mad. They were so mad that they took their madness for reality. The king drank the fresh water and was sane. But he discovered he couldn't communicate with his subjects. He had to be mad to communicate with them in order to rule them. So he had to drink the rainwater, too.

I guess I have to be like that rain king.

I started walking. I had no direction. I just started walking. I found myself up in the Hollywood Hills. I could see the city spread out beneath me. I fixed my gaze on the Sunset Tower and the Hollywood sign, and the city. Corrupted as you are, I said to it, I will conquer you! I know you now! It's between me and you now! I said to the landscape of buildings, the smog, the city. Yes, Sunset Tower, it's between me and you now! I'm ready for you now! You've taught me life's lesson. I have learned from the best! So get ready for me now! I stood there shaking my fist at the city.